Umbria

Umbria

The Heart of Italy

Patricia Clough

First published in English in 2009 by
The Armchair Traveller
4 Cinnamon Row
London SW11 3TW

This paperback edition published in 2017

Originally published under the title *Gebrauchsanweisung für Umbrien*
by Patricia Clough © 2007 Piper Verlag GmbH, München

ISBN 978-1-909961-47-0
eISBN: 978-1-909961-48-7

Typeset in Garamond by MacGuru Ltd
Printed and bound in the UK

A CIP catalogue record for this book is available
from the British Library

www.hauspublishing.com

Contents

The centre of the world

The centre of the world is a pointed greenish-white stone set in the floor of a bank on the main street of Foligno.

In the good old days, locals tell me, the centre of the world was much more fun. Then it was marked not by a stone but by a billiard pin, the red one that is placed in the precise centre of the table at the start of the Italian game of five-pin billiards. People would stand around it, chatting, drinking wine and watching the game.

For in those days, which everyone deeply mourns, the premises now occupied by the bank used to house the much-loved Sassovivo, a lovely old Art Nouveau café-bar with wooden panelling and an inviting atmosphere, where one used to meet for coffee or an aperitivo and a chat. The billiard table stood in the centre of the Sasso-vivo's back room which, according to the locals' calcula-tions, lay exactly in the centre of their town, which lies in the geographical centre of Italy – and which, as every child knows, is the centre of the world.

Alas, one day the Sassovivo gave way to a fast food joint and then to the bank. Today only the café's ornate wrought iron lamps on the terracotta-coloured façade remain to remind people of the good old days. And the stone, set beneath a round pane of glass in the floor precisely at the point where the central billiard pin once stood on its table.

It is surrounded by not one, but two inscriptions in local dialect declaring it to be 'lu centru de lu munnu'.

Some will tell you that the centre of the world – or more modestly, the centre of Italy – is elsewhere. The Romans, including such famous writers as Pliny the Elder, declared that the 'umbilicus italiae' lay further to the south, in or around Rieti, which for a time was part of Umbria. And such was their authority that for many centuries afterwards people continued to consider Rieti the navel of their peninsula. There, too, the spot was marked by a stone, placed in a square called Piazza San Rufo Centro d'Italia, with the inscription 'Medium Totius Italiae'.* Or rather, it was thus marked until one day in 1950 when someone made off with the stone while the pavement was being renewed. A plan to replace it with a cylinder sending a ray of light to the heavens was dropped for fear it would interfere with air traffic, so a stone plaque was attached to a nearby wall, bearing the message in 18 different languages.

But in the waning years of the last millennium, the Rieti town councillors decided it had to be marked in a more distinguished manner and now this 'centre' is a large, squat, round platform of travertine with the shape of Italy inlaid in the surface. It is too big for the little old piazza and I have been told on good authority that the majority of the townsfolk, like me, think it is horrid.

Meanwhile, the Italian Military Geographic Institute, which produces Italy's official maps, declared that the

---

* The middle of all Italy

true geographic centre of Italy lies further to the south-west. This one, marked by a stone carved into a spiral and topped by a slim steel peg, stands just by Ponte Cardena, a picturesque bridge that carries a Roman aqueduct across a gorge near the town of Narni. Reached after a pleasant walk along the aqueduct set in the wooded mountainside, it looks altogether more scientific. But many in Foligno and Rieti seriously doubt that science can be any more effective than local patriotism in determining the centre of a place as irregularly shaped as Italy.

These are not the only claims to centrality in these parts. What they add up to however, is that here, a good way from the sea and surrounded by mountains, lies the heart of Italy. That, and the rivalry over it, already tells you a lot about Umbria.

But being the heart of Italy, even of the world, does not necessarily mean being its powerhouse, its nerve centre, the focal point of all human activity. On the contrary, Umbria's centrality is more that of the eye of a storm, or the hole in the middle of the whirlpool. The world swirls around it but inside there is a calm, a sense of somehow being out of it all.

It is not just that the ancient Umbrians, perched on their remote, landlocked mountains, seemed to have minded their own business and had few ambitions other than survival. Or that Umbria's greatest figures, those which had most impact on both their contemporaries and on history, were also among the greatest dropouts, men and women who renounced the world and all its works. There were also times when history stormed through these valleys, bringing great turbulance but also great creativity. But then came several centuries under the notorious 'dead hand' of the Popes during which the legacies of the past and an ancient way of life remained, if not exactly frozen in time, at least reduced to evolving in very slow motion.

The 'progress' of the past half-century, bringing better roads, an embryonic airport, television, the internet and mobile phones, have not been able entirely to lever Umbria out of its time warp. The beauty of the (largely) unspoilt countryside and ancient communities, the quality and slow pace of life which are, ironically, the consequence of backwardness and poverty have in recent times become massive assets. The suffering and deprivation of their ancestors has turned out to be the fortune of today's Umbrians, even though some of the latter find it hard to grasp.

You can meet Umbrians for whom the centre of the world is boring, provincial, a place where you see the same old faces, day in, day out, where nothing much happens. For some it is even a place to flee from. And yet we outsiders, both Italian and foreign, who flip like fish out of the busy world and land in this quiet backwater, we like to think it is something close to heaven. They find it all most puzzling.

In 1999 I settled in part of an ancient olive oil mill on the fringe of an old hilltop town. One evening as I was chatting with my new friends, one of them, Giuseppe, leant back in his chair and asked: 'Patricia, what ever made you want to come and live in Umbria?' Giuseppe is an architect and has travelled, but even he was genuinely baffled. I cannot remember what I said, but whatever it was, it cannot have been anything smart. Because, as I realised at that instant, I had never stopped to think exactly why I decided to settle in Umbria, I had just known that I wanted to live here. At that moment in my life I had the rare luxury of being completely free to choose where I wanted to live, and after some searching, this was it.

Now there can be no excuse for such vagueness. What is it precisely about Umbria that so captivates one? It would be too easy just to wax lyrical about the symphony of greens and greys as the cypresses and olive trees emerge from the morning mist, the fertile valleys straight out of a Perugino fresco, the austere beauty of an ancient church, its cream-coloured stones almost luminous in the evening sunlight, its medieval cities perched on their hilltops, its incomparable paintings.

But that is only the setting. Breathtakingly beautiful though it can be, and highly important to anyone who comes to visit or live here, there is much, much more to Umbria than that.

Big sister, little sister

It was not exactly an original decision for me to make. For centuries many Northern Europeans have succumbed, first to the siren charms of Rome and Florence, then to the enchanting land in between. It probably has something to do with the *Zeitgeist*. Where Grandma longed to promenade under parasols by the sea and Mother and Father liked to hike with guitars through mountains and forests, one could say that Millennium Man's idea of paradise is sitting under a pergola eating delicious local food and drinking excellent wines, while contemplating the cypress-punctuated scenery or medieval towers and castles that one has just seen in paintings by some of the world's most divine artists. Nirvana is a beautiful old farmhouse on a hilltop surrounded by vineyards or olive groves, preferably of one's own. Failing that, there are books by people who 'did up' such houses; calenders, devoured in their millions, with every month a different arrangement of said hills, farmhouses, cypresses and vines; or at least an evening out in a restaurant with a name, food and wine from this part of Italy.

For a long time this paradise went under the name of Tuscany. This was natural: it was famous, it had Florence, the Medici, the Renaissance, beautiful villas. It only dawned on the world slowly and gently that it has another name – Umbria. Here, too, are the olives and cypresses, castles, hilltop towns, beautiful churches, exquisite paintings. Here, too, are superb wines and delightful dishes. But there is a different atmosphere. Its great buildings are often older, more austere, stonier, its art more spiritual, less worldly. Tuscany's incomparable countryside is largely man-made, Umbria's gentle cultivated valleys and hills are surrounded by forest-clad mountains, secretive and mysterious. Tuscany almost flaunts its beauty, whereas Umbria's ancient monasteries, castles, hermitages and stone villages are often hidden among rocks and dark ilex trees.

Some dismiss Umbria as a 'poor man's Tuscany'. But although pretensions and prices are certainly more modest, this misses the point entirely. Despite the similarities, and despite its long common border with Tuscany, Umbria is simply a different place with a different character, moulded by its different geography and very different history. Tuscany, and before it Etruria, the home of the ancient Etruscans, had the sea and with it contact with other civilisations, while the Umbrians lived perched on their landlocked mountains. Tuscany's golden age was the Renaissance, while Umbria had flowered earlier, in the Middle Ages. While Tuscany under the Grand Dukes, although less glorious than before, was still a player on the European stage, much of the area that now is Umbria was a dominion of the Popes, who for all the authority they may have had regarding the next world were poor rulers in this one. All independence, creativity and initiative was snuffed out, commerce and agriculture declined and the result was some 400 years of backwardness and poverty whose consequences are still being felt today. While Tuscany can dazzle, Umbria's charm has often been described as 'franciscan', austere but immensely lovable. Some will say Tuscans can seem arrogant, while Umbrians are generally modest and masters of understatement. Then there is the simple question of size. Tuscany has three and a half million inhabitants; Umbria, with 826,000, has less than a quarter of that. Tuscany is divided into seven provinces, covering a total of nearly 23,000 sq km. Umbria consists of two provinces and covers only 8,456 sq km, which makes it just over a third the size of its neighbour and one of the smallest regions in Italy.

Tuscany is chic, and it shows in house and restaurant prices and smart shops. The comings and goings of politicians and celebrities with their sunglasses and Prada bags who vacation or own houses there keeps it in the public eye. With a few exceptions around Todi (of which more later) outsiders in Umbria tend to keep a low profile and blend into the background. Apart from, alas, unwittingly raising the price of old stone houses and maybe contributing something to the economy, we have had little impact on our hosts and prefer things to stay that way. I have to admit that I first looked for a house in Tuscany. I soon gave up, discouraged not only by the prices, but also by the fact that the character of many areas has been changed by the foreigners and non-Tuscans who go there. Umbria is still an intact, Italian society. And, incidentally, any rivalry between Tuscany and Umbria exists, as far as I could establish, entirely in the heads of foreign tour operators or potential house buyers. 'We never fought each other, nor were we ever allies,' mused one colleague. 'We just accept each other.'

One might think this strange, given the tendency in the old days to go to war with the neighbours on the flimsiest of pretexts. But Tuscany and Umbria, or more precisely, their predecessor states, proved remarkably restrained in one case which could easily have provoked mayhem. In 1440 Pope Eugene IV sold a slice of Umbria around San Sepolchro to the Florentine Republic for 14,000 ducats, whereupon officials from Florence and the Papal States got together to settle their new border. They decided it should follow a little river called Rio and everyone was happy. But soon it dawned on them that in that area there were two little rivers called Rio, about 500 metres apart and that between them lay a little hamlet called Cospaia. After failing to agree how to redraw the boundary, both sides decided Cospaia was not worth going to war about and left things as they were. Cospaia promptly declared itself to be a free republic and for 400 years its inhabitants lived happily without taxes, military service or written laws while profitably cultivating tobacco, which was forbidden in most other places, sometimes on pain of excommunication. The story of what must have been the smallest republic in the world came to an end in the 19th century when Cospaia became not only a busy tobacco-smuggling centre but also a haven for draft-dodgers and other undesirables from its big neighbours. In 1825 Pope, Leo XII and the Grand Duke, Leopoldo II, re-started negotiations which lasted more than a year. On 28 June 1826 the Republic of Cospaia ceased to exist. The hamlet became part of Umbria and as a compensation for their lost freedom Cospaians were given a licence to continue cultivating half a million tobacco plants. Today, Cospaia is an insignificant collection of houses without – as far as I could see – either a shop or a restaurant. The only clues to its long independence are a yellow sign by the side of the road saying proudly 'ex-republic of Cospaia' and an inscription over its church door reading 'PERPETUA ET FIRMA LIBERTAS'.*

---

* Strong and perpetual is our freedom.

Identity

Anyone born and bred in Tuscany (unless perhaps he is a Florentine) would not hesitate to tell you he is a Tuscan – and probably feel proud of the associations with culture, wit and dynamism that the word evokes. If you ask an Umbrian where he comes from he is likely to say Perugia, Terni or whatever his home town may be. I have never heard anyone describe himself or herself as an Umbrian.

People like to tell you that this is because for some centuries this region was primarily a collection of independent cities, each intensely proud of itself and highly suspicious of, if not at war with, its neighbours. It is a habit of mind which still survives, fortunately in a much milder form, to this day. But that can also be said of Tuscany or anywhere else in Central and Northern Italy. My own theory is that besides its centrality and its other-worldliness, another defining feature of Umbria is its long history of non-existence. For many generations there was no Umbria to identify with.

Once upon a time, though, there were the Umbrians, an ancient Italic people who once spread over a good part of Central Italy from the east to the west coast and north as far as today's Romagna. They were gradually pushed back by other peoples into a small mountainous area between the River Tiber in the west and north and the Appenine mountain range in the east. A lot of the pushing was done by the Etruscans, a much more dynamic and sophisticated people who arrived on the west coast from no one knows quite where, and spread themselves out until they reached the Tiber. To the south of the Umbrians lived the Sabines, to whom they were related and whose womenfolk were famously carried off by the Romans.

It was the Emperor Augustus who first made Umbria a place name. He gave it to his 'Sexta regio' or sixth administrative area, which stretched from the Tiber to the Adriatic. Under a reorganisation a couple of centuries later, a much smaller part of this was combined with the neighbouring Etruscan lands into Tuscia and Umbria. This later got called just Tuscia and the name Umbria was forgotten for centuries. It only started surfacing again from the Renaissance, and then only on maps, not as an administrative entity. The maps disagreed as to what area the name actually referred to.

It was only in the 19th century, first under Napoleon and then under restored papal administration, that something resembling the present-day Umbria became a compact administrative entity and in 1860 after the unification of Italy, it finally became an Italian province. But even then it was an artificial construct, a patchwork. The main body of Umbria was still divided by the Tiber into two different regions which had grown out of the former Umbrian and Etruscan societies. Other areas were stuck on to these which had little in common with the rest except for their marginality and isolation. One can still see the old customs houses, large buildings with a colonnade right at the roadside, which controlled the movement of goods and people between one long-defunct administration and another. Terni, a modern industrial town with big steel industries, bombed 110 times during the Second World War, is only a few kilometres from the completely different world of the valley of the Nera with its medieval castles, convents and mountaintop villages. Orvieto, physically and symbolically separated from the rest of Umbria by the Autostrada del Sole, Italy's main north-south motorway, neither looks nor feels like the rest of Umbria. Its stone is rough, volcanic tufa instead of limestone or travertine, its links are with Rome rather than Perugia, even the advertisements posted every few metres alongside the roads, spoiling the view, are typical of Lazio and Rome, not Umbria. To this day dialects, habits and even traditional dishes vary considerably between one area and another, even between one town and another. And Umbria has always remained a somewhat fragile entity: in 1923 the Sabine area around Rieti, which is very similar to Umbria, was carved off and given to Lazio. In the 1990s an effort to abolish the whole region and split it between Tuscany and Lazio, although unsuccessful, cannot have done much for a sense of cohesion.

There is still the great dividing line of the Tiber. Some people, like my friend Theo, say that Perugians are not Umbrians at all, they are actually Etruscans. Some will maintain that even now, thousands of years later, people living in the former Etruscan area are more go-ahead, brighter, better businesspeople, while others retort that it is sheer imagination. Frankly I have not been able to detect any difference.

To an outsider, Umbrians can seem closed and reserved, particularly older people in the country areas, but on better acquaintance most turn out to be kind, friendly and disconcertingly inclined to address you with the familiar 'tu' instead of the formal 'Lei'. One might detect a lack of drive, ambition or imagination but for the most part they are reassuringly honest and straightforward, modest, dignified, and, apart from certain politicians and businessmen, lacking in guile.

Contrasts

A new American neighbour who had found her dream house almost next door to me dropped in for a coffee one day in a state of some confusion. 'I'm suffering from culture shock!' she exclaimed. 'I was shopping in the local shopping mall: I hate doing it but it is practical. This mall could have been anywhere in America, I could have been in Fresno, California. As I walked out to go to my car I saw two gorgeous little medieval Umbrian villages on the hillside. The dramatic contrast between the mall atmosphere and the lovely old communities in front of me were quite a shock to the system. It felt very strange to see these two worlds so close together.

'So I got in my car and instead of going straight home I decided to drive up and see one of the villages. It has a beautiful little church tower, peach in colour, which I wanted to see up close. When I arrived in the small piazza in front of the church, a group of women came marching down a slope towards the piazza and me. For a moment I thought they were going to run me out of town! They had cartons of soap powder under one arm and laundry under the other. They were heading for an old public wash house in the square where they set about washing their laundry by hand. No more then ten minutes before I had been in a mall where the young Umbrian women looked like rock stars ... and here just a short way up the road are these women washing their clothes in the main square. Only in Umbria!

'I drove a little further up the hill where I promptly got stuck because the street was really too narrow for cars. As if in answer to an invisible signal, people came out of their houses and guided me, an inch to the left, an inch to the right, and after an exhausting 20 minutes or so I managed to get free again. Continuing up the hill I then ran into a herd of sheep coming down. The shepherd shouted at me to get out of their way, which was impossible because there was the mountain on one side and a steep drop on the other. I just had to switch the engine off and watch the tallest sheep I ever saw go past. When they had gone I continued up the hill but the road suddenly came to a dead end. I turned around and decided that was enough for one day, I was going home! On my way down I took a different route and came past the most adorable little village. It had a tiny little church outlined in white lights. In the middle of the facade was a big 'W Maria' (Italian shorthand for Viva Maria) in bright pink neon! I burst out laughing. In America, we use W, or viva, for football teams or for visiting dignitaries!'

Umbrians have a curious and sometimes endearing relationship with modernity. The fading black-and-white photos in some restaurants or photo shops of old peasant Umbria with unpaved roads, donkey carts and muscular white oxen ploughing the land show how much has changed in the space of a few decades. And yet much still remains. The ladies in the wash house would almost certainly have washing machines at home. But given the exorbitant cost of electricity, the chance in warmer weather to wash one's sheets or curtains for free while having a good gossip with one's friends like mother and grandmother did is very attractive.

An Italian guest of mine, a city dweller from the north, came back from a drive through the Umbrian countryside on the verge of a nervous breakdown. 'What is the matter?' I asked. 'These drivers! They make me crazy,' he gasped. What he meant was not the usual Italian hazards – cars overtaking on the left, cutting in or jumping lights, traffic jams, motorcycles weaving suicidally through traffic. There is plenty of that on the main roads and he was used to it. It was the drivers one meets on the secondary roads: men (usually) of venerable age, put-putting along happily in battered Fiats not much younger than they are, usually oblivious to one's presence, but in any case unable to go any faster. Since these roads are winding and often steep, any attempt to overtake could easily end with a cross and a bunch of wilting flowers by the roadside, such as sometimes mark the expiry of other motorists in too much of a hurry. 'The only thing you can do', I had to tell him, 'is relax and contemplate the scenery. If that does not work, take Valium.' The same applies to encounters with tractors, sheep, cars driven by nuns or with little three-wheeled *Api*. The latter are effectively the motorised successor to the donkey cart and among their many devotees they are something of a cult object. They first appeared in the reconstruction years after the war as *Vespa* motorscooters with a little two-wheel trailer attached. Later they acquired little one- then two-seat cabins and have even been turned into vans, but to this day they have remained humble three-wheelers. The cheapest model, the *Ape 50*,* still has a little two-stroke motor-scooter engine that runs on motorcycle fuel and can be driven from the age of 14. These cost around 4,500 Euros, the grown-up versions fetch up to twice that much. A lot of them make a hellish noise and often give off suffocating fumes, but without them many a pensioner or part-time farmer would not know how to get fertiliser to his vegetable patch or his olives to the press.

One often feels that life here proceeds at roughly the same pace as an *Ape*. New ideas from beyond the mountains are slow in arriving and even slower in being acted upon. It is the kind of place which has re-elected the same parties to power for 60 years and does not seem to mind the rot that political stagnation has brought. It is a place where bureaucrats, building firms, post offices, and medical centres seem to think you have nothing better to do in life but wait. Where only one direct train a day links the capital, Perugia, to the nation's business capital, Milan. Where a curious kind of dippiness lurks, as in some restaurants or petrol stations whose owners never think of putting locks on the toilet doors, or municipal employees who mark out parking spaces which no car can ever use, owing to the presence of a stout tree blocking the entrance.

The past is still very close here. One might say it was still here when the Second World War ended. Then many

---

*Vespa = wasp; ape = bee

houses still did not have electricity, the roads to many towns were still dirt tracks, hill towns still did not have piped water and, as they had been for generations, were riddled with cisterns built to catch and conserve rainwater. Donkey or mule carts were still the most common means of transport in the countryside, tractors rare. Forty-five per cent of the population was illiterate. 'During my lifetime I have passed from the Middle Ages to modernity,' said my friend Dino, who had just turned 60.

When the composer Giancarlo Menotti started the Festival of the Two Worlds in Spoleto in 1958, there were only a couple of very primitive restaurants and two hotels in town, and practically no running water. Some festivalgoers who had made the, then, four-hour journey by road from Rome had to struggle into their evening clothes in their cars. It is said that even lavish applications of perfume failed to cover the smell that rose in the theatres during performances. It was largely thanks to Menotti's badgering that the town council made a decent water supply their top priority.

Most Umbrians lived off the land. But the land was owned either by the Church, religious institutions or by big landlords and much of it was farmed on very archaic lines. The peasants who worked the land were usually sharecroppers who not only did not own it, they did not even own their houses or the livestock. Half their produce went to the owner and they kept the other half. Being unschooled and illiterate they were easy for estate managers and landowners to cheat. There was no incentive to modernise or to improve the quality of the produce. How primitive it all was can be seen in the old agricultural implements they fashioned for themselves and which can now be found for sale at flea markets. Many people emigrated.

The still rare foreign visitors found it all charming, but for the Umbrians the old way of life was no laughing matter. So when things started to get better in the 1960s, they were only too glad to abandon their old stone houses in the hills and mountains and go and live in charmless, modern concrete blocks in the valleys and towns where life was so much easier. Soon the beautiful scenery painted by Perugino and others began to fill up with factories, warehouses and new homes – but who cared about that beauty when all it meant to them was hardship and back-breaking labour?

Which is why one day Tonino Metelli* decided to pull down the family's beautiful old stone farmhouse which stood close to a medieval pilgrimage church in the Valle Umbra and build an ugly concrete one in its place. The town council, to its credit, was appalled, but there was no conservation order that covered such houses in his particular area. A delegation went to try and persuade him to abandon the idea, but in vain. That house had been the scene of his and his family's poverty and suffering, he said. He hated it, it had to go. And so it went, and there was nothing anybody could do about it.

Fortunately many of the old stone houses left crumbling have been bought and restored by city folk or

---

* Not his real name

foreigners and country districts which had been practically abandoned were being re-populated – in summer at least – by Roman families or fair-haired strangers with tough hiking boots and curious accents. The Tonino Metellis who hung on to their old houses eventually found they could sell them to these strangers for far more money than they could ever have dreamed of.

Nowadays the message seems to have got through, at least on a superficial level, that the environment needs to be preserved, not least because money is to be made from tourism. But on a much deeper level there remains the conviction that it is factories, cement and acres of hideous warehouses that bring wealth and jobs and that tourists will always come anyway. The idea that such buildings could be made to blend with the scenery, be greened and landscaped, has not yet taken hold. It would seem as if Umbrians, who never could see their scenery the way others did, are blind to the urban sprawl that follows the main roads, in some places engulfing the beautiful valleys, then the hillsides and finally the old cities themselves. In this blindness lie the seeds of Umbria's destruction.

The 'ideal city'

Todi is famous. Todi is chic. Todi is expensive. One might almost say that because of its aura of international glamour, Todi is a chunk of Tuscany planted in Umbria. It owes its fame to a 'study', supposed to have been conducted by an American university professor and reported countless times in the world's press and in tourist brochures, which allegedly found Todi to be the 'ideal city' and 'the most livable city in the world'.

Except there was no such study and the American professor never said anything of the sort.

I had long been curious to know why Todi, lovely though it is, should be considered any more livable than any other old central Italian hill town. So with the help of a kind colleague from Todi I tracked down the author of the purported 'study': Richard Levine, Professor of Architecture and Director of the Center for Sustainable Cities at the University of Lexington, Kentucky. 'I never claimed Todi was "the most liveable city on planet Earth", or anything remotely like it,' he emailed me. And he explained how the whole thing came about.

Professor Levine had been to Todi several times with his architecture students working, as academic exercises, on ways to resolve the problems of accessibility in such tightly-woven medieval towns, without changing the appearance of the place. The results were exhibited in the local bishop's palace.

'Several years after these academic exercises, in 1991, I was invited to give the keynote speech at a conference in Todi town hall by a group – Agritop Umbria – that was using the conference as the kickoff event for a new regional programme in agricultural tourism,' he wrote. 'Forty to fifty journalists were invited on a two-day junket to be wined and dined and to be introduced to the programmes and opportunities that, it was hoped, would bring a new wave of tourists to a region that had been in economic decline.

'To give the conference an aura of respectability, so that it wouldn't be seen as just a tourism promotion, the organisers had invited a number of Italian academics to speak, and I was asked to give the keynote. I was not told about the commercial background of the conference and was happy to accept the offer as it was the opportunity of an expenses-paid trip to my beloved Italy.

'The title of my presentation was "The Sustainable City of the Past and the Sustainable City of the Future". It was an exposition of how Todi, like the many other towns that flourished during the *comune* period was an excellent model of a self-sufficient town that gained virtually all its material needs from its surrounding agricultural country-side ... and how this material model could serve as the exemplar for future towns that themselves could also be operating on a sustainable basis.'

Professor Levine gave the speech in Italian, '... but I don't think the journalists listened too carefully. Part of the reason was my poor Italian accent (and) I must admit that the text was a bit on the academic side.' He gave each of them a copy of his speech in Italian, 'but they had something much more interesting to pay attention to'.

'Inside the press kit given to each of the journalists, in part to attract them to attend the conference in the first place, was a summary of what purported to be an account of my research, written by a press agent who knew nothing about me or the work I had been doing. Yet he knew that in order to grab the attention of the reporters he had to create a story that would leave a strong impression – and that's exactly what he did. Although all the journalists heard my speech, had my text and many of them had interviewed me afterwards, what they really paid attention to was the press release which apparently had absolutely nothing to do with my work or presentation. I never got to see the press release but within the next week very similar stories appeared in all the major Italian new media. The story went like this:

> "Famous scientists at the University of Kentucky
> have been studying all the cities in the world and
> with the aid of powerful computers and an infinity
> of data have identified the most livable city on
> planet earth and – surprise – it is a small town with a
> population of 17,000 people in the heart of Umbria
> named Todi"

'The headlines read "Todi Most Liveable City" and "Todi Ideal City". The story spread all over Europe and on to the US. Each time it was copied from one country to the next the claims became more outrageous. Then the articles became critical. A columnist in the German journal *Die Zeit* attacked me for making such a patently ridiculous claim. Surprisingly only one journalist even bothered to get in touch with me to ascertain the accuracy of the statements that were being attributed to me. I wrote and called a number of journals demanding a retraction, but never heard back from any of them. I was very upset, both for myself as well as what effect this publicity might have on Todi.'

So what happened to Todi? When he first went there in 1983, Professor Levine said, the Tuderti, as the city's inhabitants are called, 'still had something of an inferiority complex. As Todi is surrounded by a number of more famous and more "touristed" cities – Assisi, Perugia, Spoleto and Orvieto, the locals felt that their lovely city had been overlooked. The economy was so depressed that parents had to chip in to buy toilet paper for the local elementary school.

'Before all this hubbub Todi had been the secret retreat of a large group of internationally famous artists who had each bought their decaying castles in the countryside on the cheap and had made splendid restorations. They hated all the publicity and they blamed it on me.

'But in the town it was a different story. All the "beautiful people" wanted a *pied-à-terre* in Todi and they were willing to pay for it. Four new real estate agents moved into Todi's magnificent piazza. A princess from Rome, actors from Cinecittà, wealthy people from all over bought their piece of this lovely city and converted these places, which had previously been coldwater flats, into elegant apartments. Property values increased four and five times. Construction costs rose to three times what they were in surrounding towns. And because a good percentage of the town's tax income was then based upon property values (and property value based on sale prices) the town became wealthy. Unfortunately in this process old people and poor people found it advantageous to sell their rundown flats at a high price and to buy new apartments outside the gates or at some distance from the old town, and many of the new elegant apartments were now in the hands of absentee owners. This is the way a town can die.

'On the other hand this was somewhat balanced by the upgrading of much of the town's infrastructure and a new influx of tourists, as Todi had now become an important new destination. Todi had become the envy of the surrounding towns and a new sense of pride welled up in the minds of the townspeople.'

Todi, in a way, was lucky. But it could have happened to practically any other town of its kind. 'Todi is a beautiful, very livable town, but no more so than dozens of other medieval towns in Central Italy. It is special in exactly the way in which every well-preserved Italian medieval hill town is also special.

'It is in Italy,' Professor Levine reflected, 'where one can dwell in towns that are all about living and not about the other things that have come to replace living in the modern Western cities – in particular in my own country, the US. The modern city is all about production, gaining wealth and power, speed, change and increasing consumption. What little living there is occurs at the margins.'

Looking back, Professor Levine has ambiguous feelings about what happened. On the one hand, he says, it was helpful because it brought wealth through the sale of real estate, on the other hand there are disadvantages. 'For instance, I don't view gentrification as something positive' he told me later on the phone. 'When I am back in Todi I am treated as a hero, which feels rather good. But at the same time I know I am not responsible for it.'

Nevertheless Todi, at least as it once was, remains for him and his center an important model for a sustainable city and a basis and inspiration for their development and designs of entirely modern, human-scaled communities, where there is a balance between the city's requirements and the resources of their natural environment, and between present needs and those of the future.

Water

When I look out of my windows I can see olive-clad hills sloping down to a beautiful wide valley and to mountains beyond. On winter mornings these valleys are often filled with fog and they must look very much like they did tens of thousands of years ago when they were full of water. For these wide Umbrian valleys were once lakes. The level of the water seems to have sunk progressively until by the time we have any record of them they were mainly malaria-infested marshes. The only remnant left is Lake Trasimeno, whose level was also causing much concern until recently when measures were taken to stop it sinking any further. The main roads and railways now run along these valleys, flanked in many places by industries and houses, but they are still criss-crossed by drainage channels and embankments to prevent the rivers flooding.

Now the days when I can look down at a sea of fog are getting fewer. For ever more frequently the fog swirls up above the house and right up the mountainside behind it. No one knows quite why, but we imagine it must be yet another consequence of climate change.

Water has also acted as a gigantic sculptor in shaping the mountains. Tourist brochures and guidebooks to Umbria focus mainly on the medieval buildings and art, the Roman remains and bits of the Renaissance. I had lived here for some years before I realised that up in the mountains is another, astounding dimension to Umbria, a different world, well off the beaten track and wonderul walking country. Some of it has been made into national parks but nevertheless is surprisingly under-publicised. For up there are remarkable geological formations, fascinating history, breathtaking scenery, rare wildlife and in spring an explosion of wild flowers that can rival anything in the Alps.

Over millions of years the slight acidity in rainwater has interacted with the limestone of the mountains and to carve out a karst landscape with wondrous caves, grottoes and potholes complete with stalactites and stalagmites. One can stumble upon deep hollows in the mountainside where the roof of some cave below has fallen in. On these windswept uplands, particularly around Colfiorito, above Foligno, you can find large basins which rain and snow turn into lakes or marshes in winter. Most dry out in summer, but one which does not is the marsh of Colfiorito, whose rare birds and plants have made it an internationally-important nature reserve. There are practically no surface rivers or streams, but natural ditches etched by the water and *inghiottitoi* or 'swallowers', mysterious holes through which the surface water disappears into the bowels of the earth. It is good land for sheep farming, as it has been for thousands of years, and for growing the kind of food that kept the poor going since time immemorial and which now is very 'in' – tiny lentils, flavoursome barley, spelt, chickpeas and, a more recent addition, excellent red-skinned potatoes.

An even more spectacular upland valley, the Pian Grande di Castelluccio in the Monti Sibillini, was also created by a lake. Spread out under Umbria's highest mountain, Monte Vettore (2,478m), it is beautiful all the year round, and particularly under snow in the winter. But its great time of glory is in early June when it bursts into colour as a myriad of flowers – wild narcissus, orchids, asphodel, violets, poppies and many others – begin to bloom. One is not alone there during those short weeks, but the plain is huge, much bigger than it seems when one first looks down on it as the road reaches its rim, and it is easy to get away from other sightseers. Castelluccio, at one end, is the highest village in Umbria and during the flowering season the cultivated fields at its base are dazzling stripes of colour, the red of the poppies, the blue of the lentils and yellow of the rape flowers.

Stones

The problem with history lessons at school is that they tend to be broken up into eras. One semester you study the Romans, another the Middle Ages, all neatly divided up into mental boxes. What one missed this way was the sense of continuity, the realisation that there were long periods when one era was merging slowly into the next, taking much of the past with it and remodelling it. Part of the fascination of Umbria is that you can see this flow of history all around you, starting in the mists of time and leading up without interruption to this morning. It is written in the stones.

Rough stones

There are stones that tell you that centuries before anyone started writing things down, life was lived at a much higher level than today, several hundred metres higher in fact, on these mountains. One can see round fortifications on the mountaintops, thick concentric walls of rough stones, from where the occupants could watch what was going on over a huge area below. There are several, easily accessible, in the Colfiorito area above Foligno. These were the early bulwarks of the ancient Umbrians, before they eventually moved downwards and started to live in small towns. These hill forts, or *castellieri*, were built to guard the clusters of huts, the flocks and the families in the valleys below. They may also have been religious sanctuaries and perhaps also used as pens for their animals.

The guards will also have been keeping an eye out for strangers, travellers crossing from one coast of the peninsula to the other, or heading north to south, for some of the valleys where cars now race along the *superstrade* were pretty well impassable then. On these rounded mountaintops the going was doubtless much easier and people used them to travel from the east coast to the west, or up and down the peninsula. Life in these uplands cannot have been too bad by prehistoric standards: the Umbrians could hunt in the forests, fish in the rainwater lakes, farm small bits of land and graze their flocks. And because in winter the mountain pastures were covered with snow or spoilt by frost they would take their flocks down to the lower pastures by the sea, in what is now called the Maremma, in Tuscany. Travelling in large groups for safety, they would stream down through certain mountain passes and along wide tracks at the beginning of winter, to retrace their steps at the beginning of summer. This seasonal migration still goes on today, but unnoticed: the sheep are transported in lorries.

Celestial stones

I am no archaeologist but the most exhilarating moment while exploring Umbria was my 'discovery' of the most important known Umbrian temples, on the Monte di Torre Maggiore near Terni. Of course I did not actually discover them myself, scholars and locals have long known about them and excavations have been going on, periodically, since 1984. But there is little or no mention of them in the guidebooks, and no signs to indicate their presence, which is astonishing for here at 1,121 metres above sea level, is a unique Umbrian acropolis.

It was while exploring the old Via Flaminia that I read a vague reference to an Umbrian 'celestial temple' high above the road between Terni and Acquasparta. Intrigued, I tried to learn more but only picked up snippets of information, including the fact that this steep and majestic limestone mountain was marked on old maps not as Torre Maggiore (Great Tower) but Ara Maggiore (Great Altar or Temple), that the local Umbrian tribespeople were called Naharci, and that rites performed there may have had something to do with the flight of birds.

So one sunny January day I struck off the old Flaminia just north of Terni in the direction of Cesi, a charming village of ancient Umbrian origin clinging to the mountainside. From Cesi, following signs which said only 'Sant'Erasmo', I drove on up a rough and winding mountain road, up and up, through ilex woods, past an observatory, until I came to a large open space ending in a raised outcrop of rock and on it a small, stark church. Beyond the church I experienced an astonishing revelation.

I was standing on a huge, rough stone platform which commands a staggering view over the whole sweep of the valley around Terni where the river Naia runs into the Nera, and beyond that to range after range of mountains. The platform seemed part natural, part constructed. There are great rocks which seem to have formed walls, some hewn into polygonal shapes, others simply boulders.

One can see rows of smaller stones set in the ground, and what looks like a former well. The only building was this simple, rather delapidated church. That was clearly Sant'Erasmo. Was this the site, though, of the 'celestial temple'? There was nothing to enlighten a visitor. The road continued up into the mountains but it was covered in ice and snow. Judging by the various tables, benches and stone barbecues, this promontory seemed to be a popular picnic spot in summer. But that day there was no one around and I could have got dangerously stuck, so for safety's sake I turned back.

Two months later, armed with warmer weather and the latest information about the excavations, I set off again. By then I had learned that what I was 'discovering' on this towering mountain was nothing less than the political, economic and ideological centre for Umbrians who lived over a vast area, reaching from Monte Subasio above Assisi to Monte Vettore near Norcia, Monte Soratte in the Tiber Valley to the areas around today's Todi and Rieti. Monte di Torre Maggiore is the highest peak in the Monti Martani range. The Umbrian fortress settlements that perched from 600m upwards on its various outcrops evidently controlled all the lines of communication in the whole area, probably with a huge network of watchtowers and beacons.

The flat promontory around Sant' Erasmo (790m), where people park their cars and barbecue their chicken legs, was not, as I first thought, the site of the temple. It had however been an important Umbrian settlement, a small town which became known to the Romans as

Clusiolum. The 12th-century church is all that is left of a Benedictine monastery that later stood here.

But there was more to come. Continuing ever upwards one finally reaches a point where the road becomes too rough for a normal car and there is a space to park by the side of a wood. Here are sheep-nibbled mountain meadows which merge into natural rock gardens, shady hollows with more picnic tables and barbecues and signs to guide hikers. But there is no path and nothing whatever to indicate the presence of an archaeological site. Thanks only to the advice of a hiker who knew the area, my companion and I skirted a war memorial, struck upwards through the wood, past a barbecue and then up a very steep, grassy, pathless mountainside. And there at the top, surrounded by an easily-climbable metal fence, it was.

The place is staggering. In every direction one can see over vast distances, over range upon range of mountains. On a very clear day, Dr Laura Bonomi, who led the excavations, says one can see the tower blocks of Rome some 100km away. Old people in Cesi say that one used to be able to see the cupola of St Peter's Basilica, presumably before the modern suburbs were built.

This is the highest point for many, many miles around and for a moment one can almost enter into the minds of those ancient people, for here they really must have felt closest to the heavens and the things into which they read so much meaning: the stars, the thunder and lightning, the sunsets and sunrises, as well as the flight of birds.

Around lie low walls of whitish stone. One can see clearly the outline of two temples which were both divided, like Greek and Roman ones were, into a *pronao*, or porch, and a *cella*, a walled room. The roofs were probably of terracotta tiles, for which a large pile of terracotta fragments lies at one side. They were apparently supported by pillars and the well-cut, rectangular stones also indicate that by then the Umbrians must have learned much from the Romans or maybe even used their craftsmen. The older and smaller temple was thought to be from the middle of the 3rd century BC, by which time the Romans had already colonised the area. The second, larger one has been dated as late as the end of the 3rd or beginning of the 4th century AD and among the remains was found a beautiful Greek-style head of a female statue. The remains of a much earlier temple, from around the 6th century BC, have been found underneath and may possibly have been connected to a grotto which lies below and whose entrance is on the northern side. This indicates that the site must have been used by the Umbrians as a sanctuary for nearly a thousand years. But the discovery of a flint arrowhead makes scholars think this could even have been used by earlier peoples during the Stone Age.

Deposits of votive offerings were found among the remains – stylised human figures, sometimes warriors with their helmets, or simply arms, legs or animals – which tells us that the favours the ancient Umbrians wanted from their Gods were similar to those people pray for today: injuries healed, sickness cured, husbands to return safely from war, sick livestock saved.

What divinities the temples were dedicated to, whether they were defended, where the entrance was and how people got water up there, is still largely a mystery. Dr Bonomi says there are indications that one of the gods venerated there was Jupiter, who was the principal god in the pantheon of all the early Italic peoples. It is not clear why and when the sanctuary was abandoned, although the way fragments of worked stone and terracotta were found scattered around the area indicate that it may have been destroyed with violence.

A big problem is the lack of a road to the site, says Dr Bonomi who had to walk there as we did during the excavations, until she persuaded the *comune* of Terni to let her use one of their off-road vehicles. Making a road would be difficult, not least because of the conservation laws covering these mountains. 'We really should find the original road that led here, which perhaps came from (the Roman town of) Carsulae and which must have got overgrown or erased over time.'

The Umbrians' religion, like that of the Etruscans, does not seem to have been so much a matter of personal piety or the individual's relationship with God, as the performance of complex rituals to please, placate or ask for help from their deities. An idea of these rituals, including collective cleansing (lustration) and sacrifices, is given in the seven remarkable bronze tablets written in Umbrian and found in Gubbio, the Umbrians' Iguvium, which was another sacred area. These tablets also tell us that the Naharci and some others among the twelve Umbrian tribes were hated by those around Iguvium, in fact the tablets contain a long and ferocious curse on them.

The Umbrians and other ancient peoples seemed to have believed that the will of the gods was hidden in the natural world around them, and much of their religion had to do with interpreting signs and omens. Their priests or diviners would deduce the gods' will from, among other things, the flight of birds over certain pieces of land. The idea was not to forecast the future but to divine whether a certain project or undertaking had the approval of the gods, or whether the time was propitious for it.

Dr Bonomi says this high sanctuary could well have been an *auguraculum*, a sacred spot from which the priests or diviners would observe and interpret the flight of birds. According to one theory it was one corner of a 'celestial temple' which consisted of a notional rectangle in the air. The bottom line of this imaginary rectangle ran from here diagonally downwards to another temple or sacred spot in the valley. The rest of the rectangle rose vertically from this bottom line. When important undertakings were planned, one can imagine, the tribe would be gathered here, everyone would have to remain still and silent while the priest prayed and watched. What birds passed through this rectangle, from which direction and at which height, would be interpreted by the priest as a sign of the gods' approval or disapproval.

While we were discussing this practice one day a friend who is a Latin scholar pointed out that the word 'temple' comes from the Latin 'templum' which comes from the Greek word 'temno' – to cut out. 'To cut out a section of the sky,' he elaborated. It sounds very much like what the Umbrians were doing.

These limestone mountains are riddled with caves and passages which have given rise to legends that the Umbrians had a whole subterranean city hidden inside. One has to do with a prehistoric queen who supposedly would drive her chariot through the underground streets. What truth, if any, lies behind this we do not know, but it seems likely that the Umbrians did use them. The Roman historian Titus Livius wrote in the tenth volume of his *Historiae* how in 303 BC the Romans heard of an armed band of Umbrians who, from their base in a cavern, had been raiding the surrounding countryside and sent a small expedition to put a stop to it. 'Roman troops reached the cave but it was so dark that at first they received many wounds, until they discovered another entrance ... and set fire to piles of wood at both entrances. And thus about 2,000 men who were inside the cave, forced to hurl themselves through the flames, died from the heat or suffocated by the smoke in their attempt to escape.'

It is thought that the cavern must have been here in Monte di Torre Maggiore. Local speleologists have been looking for evidence to support these various stories but results so far have been disappointing. There are certainly many caves and passages, but some have collapsed, others are practically inaccessible. It appears, though, that this area was long a bastion of Umbrian resistance against Roman colonisation.

The ancient Umbrians were not the only inhabitants of the place now known as Umbria. On the west side of Tiber were the Etruscans, a much more advanced people, about whom a good deal more is known. They left more behind them than the Umbrians, not stone houses, for they built in wood, but massive walls that still survive in some of their cities, particularly Perugia and Orvieto, and above all their tombs. The Etruscans, obsessed with death and the afterlife, built amazing mausoleums where life-like terracotta figures of the dead recline on their tombs as if engaged in some elegant after-dinner conversation. Around them was put everything they need to make them comfortable in the next world and this gives us a good idea of what their life was like in this one, with furniture carved in the rock, elegant vases, beautifully-worked jewellery and frescoes showing scenes from Etruscan life. Although they would never have admitted it, the Romans clearly had a great respect and admiration for their culture, some of which they absorbed. This did not prevent them conquering and eventually assimilating them, as they did the Umbrians.

Square-hewn stones

Some time during the 4th century BC, lookouts on the Umbrian hilltops would probably have signalled a new kind of intruder coming from the south-west into their territory. These were not travellers or merchants, but armed and well-trained soldiers. The Umbrians were no doubt thrown into great alarm, but probably did not realise that this was the beginning of the end of their world.

The expansion of the Romans into the territory of neighbouring tribes had caused fierce wars and battles. Realising they could not stop it on their own, in 295 BC the Etruscans, the Umbrians, and the Samnite tribes to the south, who had already fought two wars against the Romans and the Gauls in Northern Italy, who had once sacked Rome, formed an alliance. The two massive forces, the Romans and the Italic armies, met on the plain of Sentinum, near today's Sassoferrato in the Marche. But the Etruscans and Umbrians, whose territories were being threatened by other Roman troops, pulled out to go and defend them, thus severely weakening their side. After a long, bloody and uncertain battle the Romans eventually won and the way was open for their domination of Central Italy.

Under the Romans, stone forts and huts slowly gave way to solid paved roads, bridges, aqueducts and towns. These were not made of the rough stones like the mountain fortresses but large rectangular blocks, hewn to fit together precisely and stand for ever, unless violently demolished by enemies or earthquakes. Gradually the Umbrians were Romanised, their towns and buildings, like the temples on Monte di Torre Maggiore, came to resemble Roman ones and they got to know the pleasures of theatres, baths and organised sports. Near Colfiorito, the hut villages of the Umbrians gave way to a stone-built town, Plestia, which for all its Roman appearance was probably inhabited largely by Umbrians.

A trail of such stones marks the way the Romans came to Umbria in the very early days when they were just setting out to conquer Italy and laying the foundations for their vast empire. They needed to drive a road northeast through the Appennines to the Adriatic coast, to a future town called Ariminum, today's Rimini. This gave them access to the fertile Po valley, the Alps and the lands beyond them. In the early part of the 2nd century BC the censor Gaius Flaminius started the project, which duly got the name Via Flaminia. Solid Roman paving stones, cambered to drain off the rainwater, were laid down, mostly over ancient beaten tracks which had been used since time immemorial. And if one is driving to Umbria from Rome one can follow this route more or less accurately even today.

Beginning at what is now the Piazzale Flaminio just outside the old walls of Rome, the Flaminia heads northwards up the Tiber Valley before striking up into the hills at Ocriculum, now Otricoli, an Umbrian town friendly to the Romans. From there it continued along the hilltops to Narni. This had been an Umbrian village called Nequinum, the Romans razed it to the ground as a punishment for resisting them, and founded a Roman one called Narnia, today's Narni. A couple of centuries after Gaius Flaminius, the road was – as one might say nowadays – upgraded by the Emperor Augustus. In both Otricoli and Narni, apart from stretches of the old road itself, one can see remains of theatres, monumental tombs and acqueducts. Just by Narni there still stands one arch of the biggest bridge the Romans ever built, the Ponte d'Augusto, an astonishing feat of engineering for those days. At Narni the road divided. The busy modern Via Flaminia follows a later and more easterly route to Terni and Spoleto. But the westerly route was the original military road which the legions took into Umbria and where they left even more traces.

From Narni they headed to Casventum, today's San Gemini, whose mineral waters fed the Roman baths at nearby Carsulae, of which it seems at first to have been a kind of appendage. Carsulae was the jewel of the old Flaminia, at its height a bustling city where even visitors from Rome would come and enjoy its baths, theatres and fresh air. It was often full of legionaries returning from foreign campaigns. It is thought they would stop here to rest, recover and smarten up ready for their (usually) triumphant return to Rome – and perhaps to be monitored for infectious diseases, so they did not spread them around the capital.

No one knows precisely what destroyed Carsulae, whether it was enemies or an earthquake. Unlike many other Roman towns in Umbria it was never resettled, perhaps because this westerly branch of the Flaminia had fallen into disuse, and its ruins were plundered for building materials. What was left, however, is delightful, spread out in the open countryside, silent except for birdsong and where one can see precisely the main square, the layout of the streets, the shops, public buildings, theatres and temples.

The Flaminia continues through the Monti Martani to Aquasparta, Massa Martana, Bastardo* and Bevagna. The westerly Flaminia rejoins the easterly branch at Forum Flaminii, now a suburb of Foligno called San Giovanni

---

* Its name, a vulgar term for a person of illegitimate birth, comes from a former inn, Osteria del Bastardo, around which this unattractive little town grew up.

Profiamma, and heads off north-eastwards through the Appenines towards the Adriatic.

One major event in Roman Umbria which did not leave any stones lying around, understandably under the circumstances, was a brief but bloody visit in 217 BC by Hannibal, the great Carthaginian general, and his troops. To get to Rome, Hannibal had taken his armies through Spain and Gaul, across the Alps (where he notoriously lost most of his elephants) and was moving southwards with his army towards the city. A Roman army under our friend Gaius Flaminius was sent out to intercept him and Hannibal, who was the cleverer strategist of the two, prepared a deadly ambush. If you stand on the northern hillside overlooking Lake Trasimeno you can see all around you where Hannibal's troops lay in hiding at dawn, hidden that morning by thick fog. Below is a strip of flat land between the hills and the lake where the Romans, in marching, not battle order, were heading eastwards in pursuit of a decoy unit of Carthaginian troops. As Hannibal had intended him to, Gaius Flaminius supposed these to be the reargard of the Carthaginian forces. Suddenly the Carthaginians swept down the hillside and attacked – and within about three hours some 15,000 Roman soldiers, who could not swim, were slaughtered on that narrow strip between the hills and the lake. Another 6,000 who escaped were caught the next day and taken prisoner. Today one can walk or drive between nine points in the area which mark or illustrate aspects of the battle, see pits where Hannibal had the dead burned and get absorbed by conflicting theories of exactly how the battle was fought in the small documentation centre in nearby town of Tuoro.

Hannibal had hoped that the Umbrians and other Italic peoples would join him against Rome, but most were reluctant to do so. Instead of attempting to take the city of Rome, which would have been suicidal without more allies, he swung through the mountains to the east. There, in a valley near Colfiorito, where the town of Plestia had sprung up, he fought the Romans again. Once again thanks to Hannibal's cunning and Roman mistakes, he won. Some 3,000 Romans were killed, 600 taken prisoner and the valley got called *la palude d'Annibale* – Hannibal's marsh.

There is also a story that Hannibal and his men tried to breach the walls of Spoleto – then a Roman colony – at one of its gates. But the Spoletini poured boiling oil on to them from an adjacent tower and repulsed them. Since then the gate, rebuilt in medieval times, was called the *Porta Fuga*, the gate of flight. The trouble with this story is that Hannibal was such a brilliant general that he could have taken Spoleto if he had wanted to, and that the tower in question was only built in the 13th century, 1,500 years after the supposed event.

Hannibal continued his campaign for some years in the south of Italy but in 203 BC had to go to the rescue of Carthage which was being threatened by the Romans.

Living in Umbria gives one almost a sense of intimacy with famous ancients who had previously seemed disembodied names from a remote and inaccessible past. Tacitus (AD 56–117), the great historian whose works included 'Germania', is thought to have been a neighbour from Terni, as was the Emperor Marcus Claudius Tacitus (AD 200–275), who assumed they were related and who, during the nine months that he reigned before being assassinated, made sure that the great man's writings were widely copied. There was Gaius Flaminius whose brilliance and failings had such historic consequences. Shortly before him there was the Consul Manlius Curius Dentatus who conquered the Sabines and Terni and had the River Velino diverted so that it created the famous Marmore Falls in the Val Nerina, just above Terni. The Velino had previously run into a plain around Rieti, creating stagnant pools and swamps which presented a constant threat to the town from malaria and other diseases. So he had a trench dug to channel the river over a 271-metre cliff so that it flowed into the river Nera, thus incidentally creating the highest man-made waterfall in the world. A second Roman literary figure from these parts was the elegiac poet (Sextus) Propertius, who was born in 50 BC, possibly in Bevagna but more likely in Assisi. A third, Titus Macchius Plautus, the great playwright, was born in 254 BC in Sarsina, which was then in Umbria, but is now in Emilia-Romagna.

Holy stones
But while the Roman Empire was still apparently in full swing, men were arriving in Umbria from the middle east bringing a new religion. Jesus Christ had been crucified only a couple of hundred years earlier and already Christians, particularly men said to be Syrian monks or

ascetics, came seeking refuge from persecution in remote parts of these mountains, living as hermits, preaching His message and starting Christian communities. The Umbrians' transition from paganism to Christianity was slow and doubtless extremely difficult. Christians were persecuted and their teachers and leaders often slaughtered, only to become martyrs and saints who are revered to this day. The latter were often attributed miraculous works which no doubt originally helped convey their holiness and divine support to simple, illiterate minds. Many an Umbrian town has one as its patron saint. This metamorphosis from the ancient to the Christian era is captured in stone, for instance in the Church of San Salvatore in Spoleto where elegant Roman columns, once part of a pagan temple, are integrated into very simple Christian architecture. Or near the Fonti di Clitunno where a little building looking just like an intact Roman temple was assumed to be a relic of the days when Romans came to pay homage to the river-god Clitumnus. In fact it is now believed to have been built, perhaps in the 5th century, from bits and pieces of older temples that were lying around and from the very beginning was a Christian church, although designed along the lines of the houses of worship that people were still familiar with.

As Christianity advanced the traditions and mentality of the old world seem to have retreated slowly into ever remoter parts of Umbria, some believing that the Appenine Sibyl (the pagan prophetess who gave her name to the Appenine range known as the Monti Sibillini) was one of the last expressions of the vanishing pagan religion.

Significantly, a folk legend has it that she withdrew to her mountain retreat in a sulk because a Jewish girl called Mary, and not herself, became the Mother of God. What is claimed to be the Sibyl's cave, a large round space with seats carved out in the rock walls, a long entrance and interesting passages, still exists in the mountains just over the border in the Marche. It has never been explored archeologically and unfortunately is currently inaccessible owing to a landslide which has blocked the entrance.

But nothing illustrates Umbria's transition more amusingly than a statue in a niche on the wall of Narni Cathedral. It is said to be the 4th century San Giovenale, first bishop of Narni, possibly from Carthage and possibly a martyr. It consists of a Roman figure in classical draperies, upon which someone has stuck a head wearing a Christian bishop's mitre.

Scattered stones

By then the ancient world, already divided into a western and an eastern empire, was collapsing. The 'barbarians', Germanic tribes from the north, were closing in, the western Emperor, Honorius moved with his court – possibly along the Via Flaminia itself – from Rome to the greater safety of Ravenna and what later became called the Dark Ages descended upon Umbria. The eastern part of today's Umbria became a kind of corridor between Rome and Ravenna, which was the stronghold and main port of the Eastern Empire, Byzantium, in Italy. Wars raged up and down the land, with the Goths fighting the Byzantines who were trying to reclaim Italy, the Byzantines fighting the Longobards from the north and the Longobards fighting the Popes, not to mention sporadic appearances by Franks, Gauls and Saracens – the latter in reality Muslim raiders of indeterminate origin. The great Ostrogoth king Totila, who seems to have been honourable and humane despite his reputation as a 'barbarian,' met his death when his army was defeated in a battle in AD 552 near today's Gualdo Tadino. Towns were sacked and razed, the valleys, drained by the Romans, reverted to malaria-infested marshes, and people fled up again into the hills and mountains for safety. Agriculture, learning and art declined, roads fell into disrepair, poverty and disease were rife, the population dwindled. Ruins, more than buildings, were the legacy of these chaotic times. But there are stone witnesses which defied it all, such as the 4th or 5th century church of a former convent in Carsulae built largely with materials from the old city. Unlike the rest, the Longobards stayed, became Christians and created a large and powerful duchy which dominated much of Central Italy and had its capital in Spoleto.

The remains of ancient world became a stone quarry for building materials. All over Umbria are little old churches with Roman pillars, carved capitals, and huge rectangular blocks of travertine, often over the doors, for it would be many centuries before Umbrians would rediscover the technology of cutting and manoeuvring such large masses of stone. If the stone is marble it will have come from some Roman temple or important building, because there is no marble in Umbria and it would have been brought here by the Romans only for some special project.

Saints

One wonders how much of the ancient world would be known to us if it were not for a man born around AD 480 during this transitional period in Norcia. The town was then called Nursia, and Benedict and – it is believed – his twin sister Scholastica were the offspring of a noble Roman family. After studying in Rome Benedict became a monk and eventually founded twelve monasteries, including his greatest one in Monte Cassino between Rome and Naples. Scholastica is a shadowier figure who is said to have become a nun and perhaps founded a convent at Plumbariola, not far from Monte Cassino. Benedict was not the first Christian monk by any means, but his Rule which he recommended to his followers was widely accepted not only among Benedictines but also later orders and thus he became known as the father of Western monasticism. Although this was not their main purpose in life, his monks preserved and copied many ancient writings, and preserved them through those largely benighted centuries when so much would otherwise have been lost for ever.

By the 12th century life had very much improved. Umbria was a less frighteningly dangerous place, people could travel, trade and move down from the mountains. The population grew, merchant classes formed, towns prospered, became independent, more or less self-governing and proud – and thus developed the *comuni* or city-states which played such a great part in the late Middle Ages and the Renaissance. Stately public buildings and churches were built and artists were commissioned to paint the walls with frescoes to illustrate the message of the Christ and the lives of the Saints to the faithful who still, for the most part, could not read or write. There still was no peace, the Popes and the Emperors were still struggling for control, allying themselves with first one city, then another, while the rival cities periodically fought each other, the bigger and more powerful ones often seizing and dominating the smaller ones.

During this time there appeared on the scene a figure who was to leave a deep impression not only on fellow Umbrians but on the entire Christian world. He was born into just such a community in 1182, his father was a rich merchant, he fought in its army against the neighbouring city and lived the life of its golden youth until, whether as a result of his year's captivity in the hands of the enemy city or, more likely, a long illness, he changed his life entirely. His influence rapidly spread out from Umbria to the rest of Italy and from there to Europe and the whole world.

Whether one is religious or not, St Francis of Assisi is one of the world's most lovable figures. His message of poverty and love, his care for the poor and the sick, his humility, cheerfulness and charm, his love of nature and animals – quite apart from legends which sprung up around him – and his poetry and preachings seem to have a universal appeal.

I had sidled round St Francis for some years, unable quite to come to grips with him. Not being a Catholic or particularly religious, I wanted to know about the real man behind the object of devotion that he is for millions of believers. It was not easy. From the moment he died in 1226, well-meaning biographers, admirers and people with agendas of their own wrapped him up in so many layers of legend and interpretation that, I soon realised it was impossible for an ordinary lay person to pick his or her way through it. Quite bewildered, I begged for help from my friend Rodney Lokaj. Rodney is a distinguished medieval scholar, versed beyond belief in the Latin literature of the Middle Ages, including all the writings by and about St Francis. When he quotes them, he quotes them in the original Latin.

One day I sat Rodney down at my kitchen table, and over chicken wings, peperoni and salad he started to untangle some of the puzzle: 'You have to understand that medieval writers, in order to convey certain concepts, had to use a language that was geared to the way the medieval mind worked. For instance, the story about Francis going to Arezzo and chasing the devils out of the city – you know, those bat-like creatures you see in the frescoes – that is an allegory. In fact the city was divided into several quarrelling factions and he got the factions to sit down together and sort things out. That was portrayed as driving the devils out.

'Then there is the story of him taming the wolf at Gubbio. Since time immemorial it had been common to describe an angry, bad or dangerous person as a wolf. Like it says in the Bible: "I sent you like sheep into the midst of wolves." So it meant he pacified some troublemaker there, we don't know who, maybe some local strongman.'

But if there is one issue which illustrates the difficulty – for scholars as well as ordinary mortals – in searching for the original Francis, it is the claim that he bore the stigmata: wounds in his hands, feet and side such as Jesus Christ suffered when he was nailed to the cross.

During Francis' lifetime, Rodney says, neither Francis himself, nor his disciples nor anyone who met or saw him ever suggested he had the stigmata. Nor did they feature in any picture of him painted while he was alive or for some time after his death. So do we accept the words of Brother Elias, Francis' close disciple and, for some years, acting Minister-General of the order, who had prepared Francis' body – no doubt covered in sores caused by his way of life – for his burial? In a letter informing the Saint's followers of his death he announced 'the greatest joy and an incredible miracle' that 'not long before his death our brother and father appeared crucified, bearing on his body the five wounds which are truly the stigmata of Christ. In fact his hands and his feet were pierced as if by the points of nails which seemed to have passed through the flesh on both sides, leaving scars of the black colour of the nails. His side appeared to have been struck by a lance and often oozed drops of blood.' Or do we prefer the version of his close friend, confessor and secretary, Brother Leo, who – but only after Francis' death – said the Saint had a vision of a six-winged Seraph while praying on Mount La Verna in Tuscany and that afterwards he bore the stigmata?

That was two years before Francis died. Leo was with him on Monte La Verna at the time but did not say whether the two events were linked.

Or do we believe the official biography issued by a subsequent head of the Franciscans, Saint Bonaventure, who at the same time ordered all previous biographies to be burned. In this, Brother Elias, who had meanwhile been deposed as the head of the order for his highly controversial and disastrous leadership and later excommunicated by the Pope for siding with the Emperor, disappears entirely. According to Bonaventure the stigmata were given to St Francis by the Seraph on Mount La Verna. Were they stigmata wounds or were they, as other versions have it, actual nails formed from black flesh? And why did Pope Gregory IX, who as a cardinal had become a friend and protector of St Francis, not mention the stigmata at all in his papal bull giving his consent for Francis' canonisation or, for that matter, in further documents for years afterwards?

And these are only some of the many questions that arise from the sources on the Saint's life. An Italian iconographer and historian, Chiara Frugoni, who has studied the Franciscan question in great detail, calls it 'an impenetrable forest'. Not least of the problems is the fact that the modern concept of scientific objectivity was quite unknown to medieval writers: 'truth' was often what they wanted it to be, or what they wanted others to believe.

Bonaventure's biography had a specific purpose – to help heal the split in the Franciscan order which had already emerged during the Saint's life, between the Spirituals – who believed they, like Francis himself, should own nothing and survive by begging – and the Conventuals. The latter, who included many of the more learned members, maintained that the rule, created for a small group of followers, needed to be adapted owing to the great size of the order, the need to live in monastic houses, and to meet the practical requirements of preaching, teaching and study. So his Francis subtly changed, becoming a more gentle figure, capable of preaching to birds, less revolutionary and disturbing than he probably was, more reassuring, obedient to the Church, a man to be venerated rather than imitated, whose own life had been the perfect imitation of Christ. Hence the importance in this biography of the stigmata, the seal, as it were, of this achievement.

The great artist Giotto also joined in Bonaventure's makeover of St Francis as he painted the life of the Saint in his famous series of frescoes on the upper church of the Basilica in Assisi. Giotto's frescoes illustrated the Bonaventure biography and at the same time transformed Francis' appearance. Instead of depicting him as short, frail, with a long, but cheerful face, sticking-out ears, small, brilliant black eyes, dark brown hair and a sparse beard, as his first biographer, Tommaso da Celano described him and as earlier artists had painted him, he made Francis tall, blond and strong. And from then on Francis was invariably portrayed with visible marks on his hands and feet. This was the figure of Francis that people knew for centuries until surviving copies of da Celano's banned biographies – he wrote two of them as well as another book about Francis – were discovered in the 18th and 19th centuries.

People captivated by the personality of St Francis can be taken aback, to say the least, by what they see at Assisi. The double basilica where he is buried is huge, filled with some of the finest paintings Italian artists have produced, and certainly extremely beautiful. Less so the gigantic church of St Maria degli Angeli which dwarfs the tiny Porziuncula inside, the chapel which St Francis and his followers used and the spot close by where, in a hut of wattle and mud, the Saint died. Both seem a complete negation of everything St Francis stood for, almost an attempt to neutralise him.

Why was he awarded such vast and rich monuments which would have horrified him if he had known about them? I wanted to know. Why, indeed, did the Church embrace St Francis and his revolutionary ideas at all?

Francis, Rodney pointed out, was not the only person in his day to preach poverty and asceticism, which at the time – curious though it may seem – was actually frowned upon by the Church. The same Pope Innocent III who gave his approval to St Francis' Rule and allowed him to form an order, had excommunicated, for instance, the Cathars in France who also preached a message of purity and simplicity.

It is true that Francis had always been very careful to seek the approval of the Church for what he wanted to do. And the Pope may have felt that Francis' message and his immense popularity – he had many thousands of followers – may have been good for the Church which indeed was in serious crisis. It was riddled with corruption and had lost touch with ordinary people. But, Rodney believes, the Pope was just as concerned with Umbrian geopolitics in those days of intense hostility between the papacy and the empire.

'Assisi stands at the end of the Spoleto Valley. All the valley and the city were in the hands of the Dukes of Spoleto who were direct vassals of the Emperor. Look at the castle of Assisi, standing high above, and separate from, the town. That had been built by the Emperor in 1198 – the castle in Spoleto did not yet exist. It was the biggest castle in the area and it was aimed directly against Perugia, which was usually allied with the Popes. The Franciscan movement became necessary to the Church to combat the empire, at least on an ideological level. Francis' Assisi became a bulwark of the Church against the Emperor.'

Whatever the political calculations of his times, Francis' legacy is very much alive today while those popes and emperors are remote figures of a long-gone age. His order, albeit subdivided, is the biggest in the world with around 53,000 monks and nuns and over one million lay members. It has given the Church some 98 saints and six popes. A modern confirmation of his appeal to people of other religions, or none, is the annual March for Peace when many thousands from different nations march the 25km from Perugia to Assisi to call for peace in the world. Who knows how many realise how bitterly Perugia and Assisi once fought each other in his day.

Assisi is one of the few places in Umbria which attract crowds – Lake Trasimeno in the summer is another. Unless one is taking part in the March for Peace or some religious event the best time to see Assisi without there being too many people around is avoid religious festivals and if possible go in the early morning, in the depths of winter and on a Wednesday. On Wednesdays the groups of Catholic pilgrims which make up a large part of the crowds are usually in Rome for the Pope's blessing from his window overlooking St Peter's Square or, in summer, from the papal summer residence in Castelgandolfo, in the Alban hills to the south of Rome.

St. Bonaventure only managed to keep the Franciscans united during his lifetime. Once he died, the splits reopened and evolved over the centuries until now in Assisi one sees members of three male orders: the Friars Minor with their brown tunics, rope belts and (usually) sandals; the stricter Friars Minor Capucins, also in brown but their habit distinguished by its large hood; and the Friars Minor Conventual in black. There are the Franciscan nuns, the Poor Clares and – though not distinguishable from other visitors – men and women belonging to the lay Tertiary order who seek to live along Franciscan lines, some in the world, and some who take vows and live in religious communities.

Like Saint Scholastica, Saint Benedict's sister, Saint Clare remained then and forever in the shadow of the male saint, as was the fate of women in those times. Saint Clare was not St Francis' sister, but a young countess. She was educated, she knew the Emperor Frederick

II of Hohenstaufen, who spent part of his childhood in Assisi, and she could have been expected to marry some prominent nobleman. Instead she was totally captivated by Francis' teaching and in 1212 ran away from home to follow Francis, who cut off her hair and gave her into the care of Benedictine nuns. She was joined shortly afterwards by her sister Agnes who, like her, laid off her rich clothes and wore rough tunics to indicate that she too had accepted the vows of poverty, chastity and obedience. The sisters later moved into a little building next to the church of San Damiano where they founded what was first called the Order of the Poor Ladies, later the Poor Clares, on Franciscan lines. The Franciscan life was extremely popular among women as it was among men and just as St Francis found himself at the head of a large order, by 1238 Clare was in direct charge of between 60 and 70 convents and thousands of nuns on both sides of the Alps. She begged bishops and successive popes for years to be allowed to embrace complete poverty instead of the less austere Benedictine Rule they imposed on her Order. It was only as she lay on her deathbed that the Church finally approved her Rule, the only one devised by a woman it has ever accepted.

It takes all sorts to make holy men, and one of Francis' later followers had a completely different nature. Jacopone da Todi, or more precisely Jacopo Benedetti, had been a notary in Todi and like the young Francis had enjoyed *la dolce vita*. That is, until his wife was killed when a beam collapsed at a party and below her fine clothes they found she was wearing a penitential sackcloth, which – curious though it may seem – not even her husband knew about. He underwent a dramatic conversion, gave away all his belongings, undertook extreme forms of penance and joined the *Spirituali*, the strict faction of the Franciscan order. He first wrote violent satirical verse against the Pope of the day, Boniface VIII, and then signed a declaration that Boniface's election had been invalid, which got him excommunicated and then thrown into prison. At the same time he wrote the most passionate and powerful religious songs, called *laude* (canticles) which were among the first to be written in Italian, rather than Latin. Another great poem, which *was* written in Latin, was the Stabat Mater Dolorosa. This was eventually absorbed into the Roman Catholic liturgy and which has been set to music by many leading composers. Jacopone was never canonised but he holds a position of great respect among Umbria's collection of saints.

Lesser known, but even more possessed than Jacopone, was Angela da Foligno (1248–1309) who, after the death of her mother, husband and children all in one year, became a nun and a mystic. Her spiritual experiences became known thanks to a monk and relative who wrote them down.

Another Umbrian saint who would have been horrified by the manner of her veneration is St Rita of Cascia. Born in 1381 in the nearby village of Roccaporena, she had been very devout and wanted to become a nun but in obedience to her parents married a man who turned out to be violent and abusive. She bore this with love and patience and eventually converted him, but soon afterwards he was murdered. As her twin sons grew up she sought to persuade them not to avenge their father's death. After both died within a short time she became an Augustinian nun famous for her holiness. After she died she seemed to have answered so many prayers that she became known, along with St Jude, as the patron saint of lost causes.

Her large white shrine, built in the early 20th century, is out of proportion and out of harmony with the little Umbrian town that she made famous, but a favourite pilgrimage place for the Catholic faithful.

Possibly even better known in the modern world than St Francis or St Benedict is St Valentine, the first bishop and patron saint of Terni who is said to have been beheaded by the Romans in AD 273. Whether in fact it was he, or one of two other Christians called Valentine who were martyred in the late 3rd century, who eventually became the patron saint of lovers is not known. This does not stop Terni holding a month-long cultural festival in his honour each February where the dominant theme, inevitably, is love.

Sinners

No one here particularly loves Perugia, or Perugians, except no doubt the Perugians themselves. We go there on business, to deal with the regional bureaucracy, to see the wonderful paintings in the National Museum of Umbria, the old town, its churches and other sights, or to shop for things that are not available locally, but not because we like the place. The reasons for this dislike may seem superficial. Some people say they resent the way 'Perugia' – by which they mean the regional and provincial governments and their bureaucrats – sucks in all power and decision-making from the individual communities, Others, like me, dislike the urban sprawl and the bewildering traffic system which, unless you abandon your car at the first available car park and use the escalators and walk, can bring on severe nervous exhaustion. Umbrians are not proud of their capital city in the way that Tuscans – even those from former rival cities – might be proud of Florence. Behind it all lies centuries of violence, hatred and cruelty whose memories have still not entirely faded.

All Umbrian cities have had their saints and their sinners and Perugia is no exception. Some of its holy men and women went to great extremes – constantly flagellating themselves in atonement for their sins, or those of the world. But this city has also seen extremes of treachery and bloodshed. It has long been the biggest and most powerful, the richest and the most ruthless city-state in the region and has been at war with all the other sizeable Umbrian cities and a couple of Tuscan ones, Arezzo and Siena, as well. It was probably no accident that a special enemy of this former Etruscan city was a nearby Umbrian one – Assisi. St Francis himself as a young man joined in the Assisan army in a scrap with Perugia. After his conversion the Perugians remained impervious to his teaching and, indeed, such was the bad blood between the two communities that when St Francis fell mortally ill in Siena he was brought by a long roundabout route to avoid crossing Perugian territory and was met by an armed escort at the Assisan border – all for fear the Perugians would kidnap him or stop him returning home to die. When, after his death, his body was being ceremonially transferred in procession from its temporary resting place to the newly-built Basilica, with papal legates, bishops and local dignitaries present, it was suddenly whisked off by a unit of soldiers and, amid loud protests, locked up inside the new church. No one was allowed in until it had been buried in a secret spot deep, deep below the Basilica where no Perugian could ever reach it – so deep indeed that in the 19th century when people did look for it (legally) it took them almost two months of digging before they finally found it.

The list of Perugian battles and conquests is long and bloody. Their brutal conquest of Foligno, which was allied with the papacy, got the whole city excommunicated by Pope Martin IV. The Perugians replied by making a straw puppet representing the Pope and burning it in the main square. Much of the time, however, they were on the side of the popes against the emperors and accepted papal protection, but stubbornly refused to give up their sovereignty.

In the 14th century Perugians, like other bigger city-states, decided to pay others to do their fighting for them. They paid eight and a half florins a month, which was roughly the going rate for a soldier, more for a standard bearer and no doubt much more for the commanders. There were plenty of formidable professional warriors around willing to hire themselves out and large numbers of these were German-speaking. The first had ended up in Italy by accident. Several hundred of them had been accompanying Heinrich VII on his journey to Rome to be crowned Emperor of the Holy Roman Empire and to assert his authority over the warring Italian communes. On his way back north, Heinrich suddenly died of malaria at Buonconvento, near Siena, and the warriors were left without a master and a job. Many went home, but Tuscan cities, spotting a good opportunity, hired whole companies of them on contract, known as a *condotta,* to fight for them. The *condottieri*, as they became called, did this so successfully that the other cities followed suit – their part-time citizens' armies were no match for them. The crucial element of a battle in those days was the lance charge by the heavy cavalry, at which the highly-disciplined Germans were particularly skilled. Some of them stayed in Italy for many years but most would come for a season's fighting and go back. The attraction was not just the money, but a share of the booty, fame and honour as well. The *condottiere* who perhaps did best of all was Sir John Hawkwood, an English knight who ended up with huge feudal estates, a large fortune and fame which has lasted down the centuries. He moved among the mighty, married a daughter of the most powerful strongman of the day, Bernabò Visconti of Milan, and when he died the Florentines had the artist Paolo Uccello paint a large monumental portrait of him in Florence Cathedral. King Richard II of England asked to have his remains brought back to Britain.

Sir John is thought to have been born around 1320, the son of a tanner at Sible Hedingham near Colchester in Essex. He is believed – records from that time are unreliable and often contradictory – to have won his knighthood after distinguishing himself in the battles of Crécy and Poitiers, two of the great English victories against the French in the first part of the Hundred Years' War. It is also possible, however, that he simply took the title without permission. When the Treaty of Bretigny in 1360 put a nine-year stop to the fighting, he and other adventurers formed mercenary companies and roamed France and then Italy, fighting for anyone who would hire them and, in between wars, ravaging the countryside and terrorising the population.

By 1364 he had become the leader of the White Company, a much-feared, predominantly English band of around 3,500 horsemen and 2,000 foot soldiers thus called because of their white flags, white surcoats and highly-polished armour. They were much in demand because of their superior tactics and weapons, which had helped them win their victories over the French;

their formidable discipline in battle; and their ability to make night marches and fight in winter, which was not common in those days. Sir John was known here, since the Italians had trouble pronouncing foreign names, as Giovanni Acuto or Aguto. The Company had started off fighting for Pisa against Florence and by 1367 his reputation was such that when he and 1,000 knights accompanied the Doge of Pisa to welcome Pope Urban V at Livorno on his return to Italy from self-imposed exile at Avignon, the Pope was so terrified that he refused to disembark and continued his journey to Corneto (Tarquinia) where he was met by Albornoz.

In 1369 Hawkwood and his men were taken on by Perugia to fend off the armies of the Pope who was trying to gain control of the city. They were thrashed by a much larger papal force led by former German comrades-in-arms, or so some chroniclers have it. Others, somewhat confusingly, claim he fought for the papal side. According to some, Hawkwood was captured and later, much to the annoyance of the Pope, was freed on payment of a large ransom, as was the custom of the day. Others said he escaped and fled across Tuscany to Liguria. He appears to have returned a few years later, joined up with captured comrades who had been released by the papal authorities in Perugia and avenged himself by winning not one but two battles against his old foes. The hall in Perugia's great Palazzo dei Priori where the decision was made to release Hawkwood's fellow *condottieri* was ruefully dubbed the *Sala del Malconsiglio* – the Hall of Bad Counsel – and bears the name to this day.

Sir John went on to perform many more glorious exploits, particularly on behalf of the grateful Florentines, and even at the age of 70 was said to have 'thought and acted with the vigour of the most splendid youth'. His career was the longest of any *condottiere* and, according to one chronicler 'so well did he manage his affairs that there was little peace in Italy in his days'. While one described him as a 'great master of war' another called him 'a brigand of the first order'. And indeed Sir John was no saint. Like his colleagues, he was not above changing sides when it suited him, terrifying cities into paying him to go away, extorting ransoms, plundering and sacking towns and villages. Chivalry was by then well and truly dead and the '*inglesi*', as his men were known, were particularly notorious. Although disciplined in battle they ran riot at other times, sweeping through the countryside in Umbria and elsewhere, robbing, killing, torturing, burning homes, raping women, often in the presence of their husbands or fathers, clapping men into irons, demanding ransoms and drowning those who did not pay up quickly enough. They did, apparently, draw the line at roasting or mutilating their victims, which was the speciality of certain other nationalities. Pope Urban railed angrily against all the mercenaries, hurling excommunications against them and anyone who employed them, but it did not seem to make the slightest difference.

Perugia's, and the White Company's, defeat in 1369 spelt the end of independence. But it did not mean the end of trouble. Five years later the city rose up against the tyrannical papal legate who Urban had installed. In the meanwhile the Perugians had turned on each other in ferocious feuding and power struggles with street fights, murders, massacres and vendettas. The era of the *comuni* had given way to that of the *signorie*, rule by powerful and unscrupulous lords who often defied their nominal masters, the Popes. Among the chief figures in Perugia was a strongman named Braccio Fortebraccio (literally 'arm strong-arm') who ruled the roost for several years and the dreaded Baglioni family, many of them powerful *condottieri*, which by the end of the 15th century had eliminated rival noble families and set upon feuding among themselves. This culminated during a family wedding on 15 July 1500, thereafter known as the 'red wedding' when one faction massacred most of the rest, including the bridegroom, threw the bodies out of the windows and had them dragged through the streets. Some of the intended victims escaped. One, Gianpaolo Baglioni, returned with troops and had some 100 suspected conspirators killed and their heads impaled on spikes attached to the Palazzo dei Priori, opposite the cathedral. The cathedral, which the Baglioni had turned into a fortress, was washed down with wine and reconsecrated to purify it after the horrors. Nevertheless, successive Baglionis continued to murder and be murdered, and one, as leader of the Florentine forces, distinguished himself by selling the great Tuscan capital to the Pope, putting an end to its freedom. Finally, one Ridolfo, set fire to the Palazzo dei Priori and killed the Papal Legate. This was too much for Pope Paul III, who sent in a huge army, drove out Ridolfo, and took charge. Less than a year later, in 1540, trouble broke out again when the Pope, breaking guarantees given by his predecessors, imposed a tax on salt, doubling its price. The Perugians shut up their shops and businesses and started preparing for war. A delegation failed to persuade the Pope to abandon the tax, Ridolfo and his troops returned with a great clattering of hooves and a papal army of 13,000 men approached the city. But after a few skirmishes, as they saw the surrounding castles and villas in flames, the Perugians surprisingly lost the stomach for a fight and caved in. This time the Pope had the Baglioni's houses torn down and built a formidable fortress over them as a symbol of his might.

In between battles, feuds, conspiracies and the like, the Perugini would amuse themselves with stone fights. Teams armed with stones would fight each other for possession of town squares. Despite heavy padding, the 'game' would end with several corpses strewn on the ground.

With the building of the Rocca Paolina, the Church reasserted its control over Umbria in earnest and thus began the long hibernation under what Umbrians call the 'dead hand' of the papacy. Trouble broke out again towards the end, in the revolutionary year of 1848 when the Perugians tore part of the loathed Rocca Paolina down. Eleven years later they chased the Papal Legate out of town, the Pope sent in Swiss troops and not only Perugian soldiers but innumerable defenceless citizens were massacred in the most appalling atrocity yet. The Rocca, which had been quickly rebuilt, was finally torn down for ever in 1860 when Umbria joined the rapidly-unifying Kingdom of Italy and the legendary *Bersaglieri* marched in to replace the Papal troops. Only its foundations and the remains of the Baglioni houses are left, in underground passages and halls which one can see as one takes the escalator from the Piazza dei Partigiani car park to the centre.

More stones

The mayhem in Perugia has taken us into the 19th century and far ahead of ourselves, because to appreciate Umbria's great flowering, the era which so shaped its character, we have to go back to the Middle Ages, to St Francis' time. This flowering can still be seen all over Umbria, in the city squares, the monasteries and churches, and in buildings scattered around the countryside. One way to get a concentrated taste of that far-off world, and its legacy over subsequent centuries, is to explore the Val Nerina, the valley of the dark, limpid River Nera.

This is a narrow valley, quite unlike the open, sunlit Valle Umbra nearby, with steep, wooded mountainsides. Its atmosphere is secretive and mysterious and one can feel almost lost in time. At almost every turn is a castle, a watchtower, a stone village within its old walls, clinging to the hillside, roads leading to others high up, out of sight, and everywhere ancient churches, many containing beautiful paintings or sculptures. Now it seems remote from the mainstream of life, despite its nearness to Terni and the modern tunnel which links it with Spoleto. But in medieval times, and even earlier, it was a lively thoroughfare and a thriving civilisation centred on the large monasteries.

The most beautiful and fascinating one, in my view, is the Abbey of S. Pietro in Valle. If you approach the

Val Nerina from Spoleto, turn right after the end of the tunnel and join the main road that runs alongside the river in the direction of Terni. As you near Ferentillo look out for signs on the right to S. Pietro in Valle. There are two approaches from the road, both lead into a beautiful, wooded, silent side-valley and end in the tree-shaded car park.

The scene is so peaceful that it is hard to imagine that these monasteries were great political, economic and cultural centres in their time and that there must have been much coming and going along these rough lanes.

Here one really can get a sense of the continuity of history, from the time it was a place of pagan, presumably Roman, worship, to around the 4th century AD when two Syrian monks, said to have been called John and Lazarus, fleeing persecution, came to live and pray in caves on the hillside and built a small oratory. By the 8th century the region was part of the Longobard Duchy of Spoleto and its ruler Faroaldo II, as instructed in a dream, built a church over the graves of the two hermits. In AD 720 after being deposed, it is said, by his son, he became a monk and turned San Pietro into a Benedictine monastery. It was subsequently sacked by marauding Saracens, restored around the year 1000 and was decorated with some of the most wonderful medieval frescoes in all of Italy. Eventually S. Pietro declined, was abandoned and fell into ruin. It is said that what we see today was saved thanks to a shepherd who kept his sheep in the ruined church at night. Although illiterate, he realised instinctively that the fading frescoes were something special and – we don't know how – put in motion a process which led to its restoration during the 20th century. One can still see Faroaldo's tomb, a 3rd century BC Roman sarcophagus, the old altar, a rare and beautiful piece of Lombard craftsmanship, pillars, lintels and carvings from Roman times. Some of the frescoes are irreparably damaged, others are undecipherable but the rest are splendid.

It is a good idea to go in the morning because then the church is open to the public and one can wander round usually undisturbed. Ask the lady caretaker if she would kindly open the door on the south side of the church. The ostensible purpose is to see two Lombard carvings in stone of Saints Peter and Paul which at some stage were built into the door supports, but it is also the only way of seeing the charming cloister, because the monastery area is now a hotel and it is inaccessible to non-guests.

A morning visit has a second advantage, which is that one can lunch in Il Cantico, the restaurant on the car-park side of the building. It is risky to say this because such establishments can change so fast, but at the time of writing it is one of the best restaurants in Umbria and easily my favourite.

A third advantage is that after lunch one can drive a little way further on in the direction of Terni and see the Marmore Falls which of course are not medieval but the work of ancient Roman engineers and which are usually switched on for tourists' benefit at four in the afternoon (though it is worth checking the time). Anyone who, like me the first time I saw it, expects a sudden mass of water to come plunging down the mountainside will be disappointed. They are opened and closed slowly, but in full force are spectacular.

If, instead, you turn left after the tunnel from Spoleto (or retrace your steps up the valley from S. Pietro) and head in the direction of Visso you will eventually see a sign to Cerreto. Not Borgo Cerreto, which is on the road, but the little old town around its castle up on the mountain which has left us a curious legacy. In the Middle Ages Cerretans would travel all over Italy and beyond, begging for alms on behalf of medical or religious institutions – who knows, possibly for the Benedictine Abbey of Sant' Eutizio which we will come to. When the Council of Trent put an end to this kind of begging, from which the Cerretans presumably got a cut, they found another, probably very lucrative, way of making money. They devised all sorts of unguents and powders and travelled around, both in Italy and abroad, selling them at fairs, markets and in town squares over Europe, accompanied with a fast patter in obscure, pseudo-medical language, especially when people complained that the cures did not work. And it is from their name – *cerretani* – possibly influenced also by the word *ciarlare* – to prattle, that emerged the word *ciarlatani,* quacks. This passed into French and then into English as *charlatan*.

A little further on you come across much more serious early medicine. It began in the lovely Benedictine monastery of Sant'Eutizio on the mountainside just after the little town of Preci. Like S. Pietro in Valle, its history goes back to Syrian anchorites who lived in caves in the nearby mountains and formed a little community. When their first leader, or abbot, Spes, died they chose a particularly saintly colleague, Eutizio, as his successor. Eutizio's reputation for holiness was such that with the gifts of admirers the monastery grew until it too became a highly influential centre for the area. One of the monks' specialities was healing. They made medicines from herbs that grow in the valley and would perform surgical operations. But in 1215 the Pope forbade monks and priests to cut people up. Anxious not to let their skills be lost, the monks taught them to the people of Preci. They proved to be good pupils because, living within the orbit of Norcia, whose hams and sausages were famous (as they still are), they were already skilled in the castration and butchering of pigs. These surgical skills were passed from father to son without the benefit of university medical studies. The Preci surgeons were specialised particularly in operations on cataracts, gallstones, hernia and haemorrhoids. They invented and made their own surgical instruments which were apparently well ahead of their time and were used by other surgeons centuries later. They developed primitive, but apparently effective methods of cauterisation, disinfection and narcosis. Although not as famous as the surgeons of the early Salerno and Montpellier medical schools, they were well known internationally and are reputed to have operated on celebrities such as Pope Sixtus V, the Sultan Mehmet the Conqueror and Queen Elizabeth I of England. I regret to say that another speciality was castrating choristers so they would keep their pure, high voices.

Some thirty Preci families made a very lucrative living this way and it shows in the elegance and quality of their houses in this hilltop town, particularly in those of the most famous and successful family, the Scacchi, who among other things were eye doctors to the French royal family. There is a small museum dedicated to this early surgery in the Abbey of Sant'Eutizio.

Papal stones

Driving northwards along the Flaminia through the mountains from Terni, you round a certain bend in the road and suddenly the mighty, ivory-coloured castle of Spoleto bursts into view. It is both beautiful and awe-inspiring, standing on its peak overlooking the city, visible far down the long Valle Umbra at whose southern end Spoleto stands. You will have passed another like it, high above the city of Narni. In Orvieto stands another. At the further end of the Valle Umbra is yet another, crouching on the hilltop above Assisi, frowning at Perugia, and much bigger and stronger than the one St Francis knew. Romantic and obsolete they may seem now, but when they were built they were formidable and marked an important moment in Umbria's history.

These great castles are the legacy of Gil Alvarez Carrillo de Albornoz, a Spanish cardinal, military commander and diplomat, in a first and temporarily successful campaign to restore Papal authority over the Church's possessions. The Popes and their court had been residing in Avignon, in what is now southern France, since 1309, but were under strong pressure to return to Rome which had fallen into decay in their absence. But first they had to establish law and order. In 1353 Urban V dispatched the capable Albornoz to Italy where, with a mixture of diplomacy, persuasion and military might, he restored a semblance of peace. He built (or, as in the case of Assisi, rebuilt) many fortresses all over Central Italy, not only Umbria, some of which have disappeared or been changed out of all recognition. One city after another in Umbria, Tuscany and elsewhere bowed to him or was defeated and usurping strongmen were vanquished so that in 1377 Urban was able to embark on the journey back to Rome. Albornoz welcomed him in Tarquinia, then called Corneto, on the Tyrrhenean coast, in a magnificent ceremony during which delegations from all the Umbrian cities except Perugia handed the Pontiff the keys of their gates. Shortly afterwards representatives of the city of Rome did the same. But the situation along the coast was still so fraught that it took four months to put together an army strong enough to escort the Pope safely to the ruined city.

Albornoz died the same year and so did not live to see the Pope and his court return not long afterwards to Avignon for a few more years, or learn that the order that he had created in Umbria and elsewhere had fallen apart again.

With all the insecurity, violence and bloodshed in Umbria and elsewhere at the time, it seems incredible that art and culture could have flourished. And yet that era – we have now arrived at the Renaissance – produced Umbria's greatest painters. Until then Umbrian painting had been simple, spiritual and medieval in style. It was the influence of Florentine and Sienese painters that sparked a burst of great creativity, and particularly Fra Filippo

Lippi who, reputedly exiled from Florence by Lorenzo dei Medici for immorality, painted a series of scenes from the life of the Virgin Mary in the great apse of Spoleto Cathedral. Another was Benozzo Gozzoli, and his three tiers of frescoes depicting the life of St Francis in the Museum (formerly Church) of St Francis in Montefalco.

The most Umbrian of them all, although he was trained in Florence and worked for a long time both there and in Rome, was Perugino. Perugino was not born in Perugia but in Città della Pieve, and his real name was Pietro Vannucci. His luminous, serene, almost dreamy paintings in pastel shades seem a world away from all the murder and intrigue. The bucolic Umbrian landscapes, with verdant valleys, sometimes a lake, and gentle hills with the odd rock or trees, that serve as background to his crib scenes or martyred saints, are beautiful and tranquil, populated only by shepherds or a few horsemen. One would never imagine that bloody battles had ever been fought there. Many of his major works are now in the world's great museums but a number remain in the Galleria Nazionale in the Palazzo dei Priori, where the heads of supposed conspirators were impaled and which Ridolfo Baglioni once set on fire. Others are dotted around Umbria in churches and museums, usually well-signposted.

There are fewer works left here by Raphael who, although not an Umbrian – he was born in Urbino over the mountains – spent his formative years in Perugia apprenticed to Perugino. Spotted by Pope Julius II, he was called to Rome to paint rooms in the Vatican and spent most of the rest of his life there, working for the

Renaissance Popes. Another distinguished pupil of Perugino was Perugia-born Bernadino di Betti, better known as Pinturicchio who, like Raphael, did most of his important work in Rome. His main works in Umbria include the Baglioni chapel in the Church of S. Maria Maggiore in Spello and frescoes in Spoleto Cathedral.

A less well-known pupil was Giovanni di Pietro, known as Lo Spagna because he was born in Spain. Like Pinturicchio his style owes much to Perugino's influence and, fortunately for the Umbrians, much of his work remained in the region.

The Renaissance left not only paintings but also a fair amount of stones in Umbria. Its greatest jewel is the church of Santa Maria della Consolazione just outside the walls of Todi. A masterpiece of Renaissance architecture, it is believed to have been designed by Bramante, the architect of St Peter's Basilica in Rome. Topped by a dome, it is built in the form of a symmetrical Greek cross and strikes one as a triumph of geometry. This type of cross was also Bramante's original design for St Peters, before the west side was lengthened to create a nave.

Umbrian noble families rebuilt or redesigned their palaces in Renaissance style, often remodelling medieval buildings and giving them elegant new facades and entrances. But somehow the Renaissance did not take over as it did in Tuscany. With their narrow, jumbled, often dark streets and alleys winding round their hills, rather than being laid out on an open, geometric pattern, the Umbrian towns remained predominantly medieval in appearance and atmosphere.

Hilltop towns

Umbria has 92 self-administering *comuni*, tiny, small or middle-sized. The smallest, Poggiodomo, has 172 inhabitants. Even the biggest, Perugia and Terni with roughly 160,000 and 100,000 inhabitants respectively, are small compared with most other modern Italian cities. Many of the *comuni* are very old, and a fair number of them are perched on the tops of hills where it has always been safest. Their stories can be read from their stones, rather as one can tell the age of a tree from the concentric rings in its trunk. Only one has to look from the bottom up, rather than inside to out.

Somewhere in the town, though not always surrounding it any more, will probably be the old defensive walls. The huge, solid blocks at the bottom, where they fit onto the rock, are often Umbrian or Etruscan, topped by more refined ones, with Roman arches, put there when the Romans came. There is a famous and impressive Etruscan arch, though, *l'arco Etrusco*, in Perugia. It is a high and stately arch which was renovated by the Romans when they captured Perugia after a long siege and into which was carved its new Roman name, Augusta Perusia. They also saw to the more finely-worked and well-fitted stones in the upper half of the two flanking towers while the rougher ones below are Etruscan. On top of one of the towers is a graceful Renaissance loggia

Underneath the asphalt or cobbles in the streets where you walk may well be large Roman paving stones with ruts carved by a thousand cart wheels. Since Umbrians have tended to rebuild their little cities rather than replan, the layout of the streets in some places – like Bevagna and Foligno – is still the original grid pattern laid down by the Romans: in Spoleto the market square lies over the Roman forum. Building work under old town houses sometimes turns up Roman foundations and mosaic floors. From the centuries after the fall of the Roman Empire there are some early Christian buildings and fortifications, although, as I have said, those times specialised in destruction rather than construction, and some of them served as foundations to be built on again later. But of the Middle Ages there is usually plenty, starting with the stately town halls and other administrative buildings, churches, convents and tall houses crammed together whose upper stories jut out over lower ones. When a town was devastated, whether by enemies or earthquakes, people tended to build on top of the rubble rather than clear it away, so the streets and houses became higher than the original level, which often explains the curious tops of arches to be seen in the facades of houses along the streets in, for instance, Assisi.

One sometimes wonders how such small towns could have such a remarkable number of stately *palazzi*, or 'palaces'. But while the majority of Umbrians were poor, some people were very rich. The biggest houses, and some are exceedingly big, were usually the headquarters of the powerful families like the Baglioni who took power after the *comuni* failed. Others were the homes of wealthy land-owners with their large families, dependents and servants, or of top officials in the Papal administration who had used their position to enrich themselves. Often they built themselves fine summer villas in the countryside, sometimes only a few miles away, where no doubt the air was fresher and more salubrious than in the narrow alleys of the towns. For centuries the more powerful families ruled the roost, building themselves roads and churches and their leading members running the community as magistrates or mayors. Others took orders and became priests, bishops or superiors of monasteries, yet others went into the legal profession, or became gentlemen scholars, writing erudite essays on historical or other topics in their frescoed studies. Between them and the many humble sharecroppers on whose labour they lived, was very little. There were artisans and shopkeepers but few schools, and Umbria lacked a flourishing middle class to develop businesses and trade.

In those days there was more life in the streets than there is today. These towns, in fact, are where most people lived, rather than the suburbs of cities like today. Craftsmen worked and little shops thrived where now there are long-closed shutters. The churches were full and there were frequent processions through the streets. There were big markets, particularly livestock markets when all the farmers would bring their animals from miles around. Life was lived outside; people met, talked and sat in the streets and piazzas. Most people knew each other and many were related to each other, and it is much the same today.

These streets are still enchanting, with their arches and picturesque corners, and especially in summer with the play of light and shade. But a stroll through the town often makes me very sad, especially in winter when icy winds slice through the narrow alleys and there is no one, but no one around. The big *palazzi* stand empty, often abandoned, their high frescoed halls echoing to one's footsteps, their courtyards full of weeds and grime. The children and grandchildren of those who once ruled the roost have gone into the professions, into politics or business, left town and moved to the big cities. They return, if at all, only for short periods in the summer. Some *palazzi* have been converted into apartments and are sometimes ruined in the process. A few are used for cultural purposes but many are slowly decaying. Unless the old town has some means of attraction, like Assisi or Todi, it is likely to slowly waste away while the town council racks its brains to think of ways of bringing people back again. Where a couple of thousand once lived, now perhaps a couple of hundred, predominantly old people. Shop after shop has closed down, unable to compete with the supermarkets in the valleys. 'It's so good to see you, Patricia,' exclaimed one neighbour as I walked the dog along the street one winter's day. 'There used to be so many people around in the old days. I was just thinking that it is so empty here I could drop dead here in the street and no one would know.'

Abandoned, too, were many of the sharecroppers' ramshackle farmhouses, especially the more remote ones, as the poorer people emigrated, some to the big cities, many abroad. But these houses have found saviours, often the fairhaired foreigners for whom the scene of sharecroppers' misery is the house of their dreams. Even though they may be used only in the summer, the houses have been saved – albeit sometimes insensitively 'done up' – and the country districts at least partly repopulated again.

Life now, or much of it, takes place in the valleys and the modern areas around the old towns. Stones have given way to concrete, airbricks and plaster and huge numbers of anonymous prefabricated buildings. And here lies the great problem, for 'modernity' in the shape of factories, outlets, supermarkets or high-rise apartment blocks, has been imported thoughtlessly, without any attempt to adapt it to the Umbrian environment. Many people are not bothered by this: when your family has never had its own house and hated the land on which it had to work, you do not care – you do not even see – what is happening to the environment. The mentality from the past is threatening to destroy the Umbria of the future.

In the first years of this century, it finally dawned on the politicians that Umbria has a huge asset in its still partly unspoiled environment. At the same time they realise that many of the industries which helped pull the region out of agricultural poverty are now being seriously threatened by globalisation. The government brandishes the slogan 'Umbria – the green heart of Italy' *ad nauseam* and conservation and tourism are now its declared priorities. But the unhealthy symbiosis between entrepreneurs and administrators and a cement-equals-wealth mentality means that these often remain empty words and building goes on as before. As a result environmental protest groups are springing up in *comuni* all over Umbria, of which more later.

Yet life in the little old towns is far from melancholy. Once I settled here I was astonished to find that, if I put my mind to it, I could go to concerts and the theatre almost as often as if I lived in a city. The little old theatres supported by the nobility, veritable jewel boxes where once leading opera and theatre companies would perform, are still open and active. They have plays, performed by professional as well as amateur groups, jazz concerts and classical concerts – all in miniature and mostly with regionally, rather than internationally, famous musicians – but the standard is remarkably high. The beautiful old churches, and, in summer, the cloisters of convents, are also wonderful settings for more concerts. Spoleto has its Experimental Opera Theatre whose high-level competitions, two-year courses and opera season give budding opera singers valuable practical skills after they have completed their singing studies and help launch their careers.

Umbria is also the home of talent in all sorts of unsuspected areas, for instance in organ building. Marvellous old organs, often covered in dust, have been discovered in the lofts of little old village churches. The town of Amelia has seven, and there are another eight in surrounding villages. They were discovered by a Dutch organ specialist, Wijnand van der Pol, and many have been refurbished. Mr van der Pol's unearthing of these treasures led to the formation of an Organ Academy which holds courses and seminars on organ playing, a music school, and an organ festival each May. Organ building is still alive and well: after the 1997 earthquake, the old family firm of Pinchi from Foligno restored the old Renaissance organ in the church of S. Francesco in Trevi, which is dated 1509 and is claimed to be the second oldest in Europe. The deconsecrated church had served in the past as a granary; the organ was covered in flour and dust and was long thought past saving but in a labour of love lasting seven years Pinchi was able to restore it to its original state. Pinchi has also reconstructed a claviorgan, a remarkable instrument combining, as the name suggests, a clavicembalo and a small organ. It was not some fantasy – claviorgans existed around the 16th century and music was written for them. Some can be found in museums but they did not get used widely, possibly because of tuning problems, which is a pity because the combination of sounds Pinchi's instrument makes is truly beautiful.

It does require quite an effort to be informed of the various cultural events in the different towns as they are often badly publicised, particularly outside their own territory. Far better known and publicised are Umbria's two big international events, Spoleto's Festival of the Two Worlds and Umbria Jazz.

The Spoleto Festival was the brainchild of Gian Carlo Menotti, the Italian composer who refused to knuckle under to the Fascists and fled to America to pursue his career there during the war. It was a pioneering effort in those days, combining international pizzazz with a splendid old town that was threatening to dwindle into a museum piece. The Festival sparkled on the European post-war scene; it was innovative, it brought American and European performers and artists together, and in its heyday it was very chic. Everyone went there, Brigitte Bardot, Sophia Loren, the poet Ezra Pound, Britain's young Prince Charles, Elizabeth Taylor and Richard Burton, Alan Delon, Romy Schneider, all pursued by the paparazzi cameramen of the day. Nureyev danced, the young conductor Thomas Schippers made his name, Luchino Visconti directed plays. The American beat poet Alan Ginsberg was temporarily detained and charged for reciting 'obscene' verse, and the whole town held its breath in alarm as Louis Armstrong suffered, and survived, a serious heart attack. Henry Moore, Alexander Calder and Giacomo Manzu exhibited sculptures, Christo wrapped the fountain in the Piazza del Mercato, not realising – despite angry protests from the husband – he was also wrapping a tiny apartment where a woman was on point of giving birth. An ambulance, sirens wailing, arrived just in time before she suffocated. The Bishop of Spoleto protested in vain about Salomé embracing the bleeding head of Jokanaan in the last act of *Salomé*, and again at topless African dancers. To pacify him they covered their nipples with little flowers, which then kept falling off.

As the amount of summer arts festivals increased, competition got tough, and as Menotti aged the Festival's glory faded and the direction gradually passed into the hands of his adoptive son Francis. The programme became more mainstream, the organisation left much to be desired, performers were often confronted with row upon row of empty seats and the Festival's finances, which had often been shaky, were causing much concern. Sadly, Menotti died at the age of 95 on 1 February 2007 just at the start of the Festival's 50th anniversary year. By then its debts had reached around five million Euros. The city council ousted Francis Menotti and brought in new management. Whether it will succeed in putting the festival back on its feet remains to be seen.

In summer, mostly, but also spring and autumn, the sound of trumpets and drums reverberate through the piazzas as many towns and villages give themselves over to medieval or Renaissance jollification. There are costume processions, pageants, *palio* races, whether with horses or handcarts, various forms of jousting, archery with longbows and crossbows, flagwaving and ancient music. Bevagna puts on the *Mercato delle Gaite*, when townsfolk recreate the old craftsmens' workshops of yore. Self-taught and remarkably authentic-looking, they show visitors exactly how candles were once made, how parchment, ink, pen and old musical instruments were crafted and how potters and dyers used to work. Some places go back in time, making whole streets 'medieval' again and reenacting long-vanished scenes, including medieval torture chambers and brothels.

Most of this is completely phoney. Some of the festivals were started during the Fascist era when the regime was busy rediscovering, or reinventing, Italy's past, but most were thought up at some stage since the war. Only a few festivals are genuinely old, the oldest and most famous one being the *Festa dei Ceri* in Gubbio whose origins go so far back in time that no one really knows whether it started as a pagan festival in honour of the goddess Ceres or whether it evolved from a procession in honour of the town's patron saint, St Ubaldo, in 1160. Three teams, followed by the entire population, race at top speed, balancing perilously tall octagonal structures, the *ceri*, through the steep, winding streets of the town, ending in the cathedral. People throw themselves into the festivities with immense gusto. Towns reverberate for weeks beforehand with the sound of drummers practising their rhythms. Inhabitants go about unselfconsciously in tights and tabards or long skirts and wimples, and one notices how well Birkenstock sandals go with rough peasants' tunics. Many of these events were doubtless thought up originally for the benefit of the tourist trade, but one gets the distinct impression that the locals do it primarily for themselves, and if tourists want to watch, then so much the better.

But those are only one kind of festival. There are also the religious ones, particularly for the local patron saint's day, and finally the *Sagre* dedicated to the local speciality, whether it is the eel, the bean, celery, or the snail. Whatever the excuse, the whole family turns out – children go to bed very late in Italy. There is folksy music and dancing – and here the *liscio*, the real old ballroom dancing, comes into its own. Many a no-longer-young couple puts on evening dress for the occasion and addresses themselves very seriously to the business of foxtrotting around the dance floor. And whatever the reason for the jollification it invariably ends at table – long wooden trestle tables where the local menfolk and young people bring local wine and hearty traditional dishes cooked by the wives and mothers in nearby kitchens. One really feels very close to the soul of Umbria.

When the earth shakes

A las, throughout the ages many of Umbria's buildings have been reduced to rubble or badly damaged by earthquakes. Whole towns and villages have been flattened, some of them several times, and many, many thousands of people killed by this periodic scourge. On 4 June 217 BC, according to Roman historian Titus Livius, there was an earthquake which 'overthrew large portions of many of the cities of Italy, turned rivers and levelled mountains with an awful crash'. But in the heat of the terrible battle that was in progress on the shore of Lake Trasimeno at that very moment, neither Hannibal's nor Gaius Flaminius' troops appear to have noticed it.

Earthquakes have indeed changed water courses, including the *Fonti di Clitunno*, the springs which flow from the foot of Monte Sorano to form the small, crystal-clear lake at Campello near Spoleto. In ancient times these springs were once much more abundant, the river navigable, the pond larger and the whole area a holy place dedicated to the river god and oracle Clitumnus. It was surrounded by temples, villas and spas and one of its visitors was the Emperor Caligula who came with his court by boat to consult the oracle. But in AD 446 an earthquake drastically reduced the flow of the springs and the area lost its appeal. Despite the busy Via Flaminia just next to it, it remains an unforgettable beauty spot with its small islands, poplars and weeping willows, praised by more recent poets and writers as well as Roman ones.

Earthquakes can be terrifying experiences. They often start with a loud roar or rumbling sound and a shaking or pitching of the earth. People run out of their houses for fear of being buried under them. Towers, walls, whole buildings can collapse, often even lightly-damaged ones become unsafe to live in. Most people prefer to live for a time in tents, mobile homes or cars, fearing more shocks to come. The death toll depends to a great extent on whether there were lighter shocks at first which enabled people to get to safety, or whether a violent one occurred without warning.

In 1298, in the area of Spoleto, the shock was so violent, according to a contemporary account, that people were thrown to the ground. The aftershocks continued for about six months, which is not uncommon, and one can imagine the state of the inhabitants' nerves during such a time. In 1328 the town of Preci, according to another contemporary report, was destroyed so completely 'that not a single man or animal remained alive'.

Norcia has been devastated five times by earthquakes. Fifteen were recorded in Spoleto up until 1900 alone. Reconstruction after earthquakes always gave Umbrians a chance to 'modernise', with the result that in several towns the cathedral or other churches may have beautiful medieval exteriors but baroque or neo-classical interiors which are far less attractive to our 21st century eyes.

Over the centuries Umbrians have reported seeing chasms opening in the mountainsides during earthquakes, of sighting flames, of the water in wells sinking or rising dramatically, water turning white and the appearance of huge quantitites of dead fish in Lake Piediluco. Friends who witnessed a big daytime shock during the last earthquake said that everything around them changed colour and became grey.

I had not yet settled in Umbria at the time. That was in 1997 when 11 people were killed, 126 injured, 23,000 made homeless and 90,000 buildings were damaged. Some villages were devastated. The old centres of towns like Nocera Umbra and Massa Martana had to be evacuated. Some 100,000, fearing further shocks, temporarily fled their homes.

The best-known victims, though, were Umbria's cultural treasures, starting with the great Basilica of St Francis at Assisi where part of the vault collapsed, destroying a fresco by Cimabue. Stately old *palazzi*, beautiful churches, frescoes, and many many homes were damaged, often seriously and many Umbrian towns and villages remained wrapped in scaffolding and topped by huge cranes for years afterwards.

My next-door neighbour told me that she woke to the noise as of a huge lorry thundering past and our old olive oil mill rearing and plunging like a ship in rough seas. Some friends described how they leaped from their bed in terror, could not find their way out of their mosquito nets in the dark and were flailing around frantically. It sounded funny afterwards but it was terrifying at the time. Looking back, people remembered strange signs which presaged the earthquake, although they did not realise it at the time: a friend's hen flatly refused to let herself and her chicks be shut in the hen-coop that night, and a hedgehog, seeking refuge in my neighbour's art studio, got caught up in masking tape and had to be picked free.

Umbria's study of its earthquakes is about as Umbrian as anything could possibly be. The Perugia Seismic Observatory is housed in the thousand-year-old basement of the Abbey of San Pietro and run by Benedictines. No sign announces its existence, and you could wander for hours through the various cloisters – the monastery later became huge – without finding it, not even the university students studying agriculture in much of the rest of the building are aware of its presence. Yet it has been a powerhouse of scientific investigation. In the 17th century Don Benedetto Castelli, a favourite pupil and collaborator of Galileo Galilei, invented the *pluviometro* here, to measure rainfall. Other scientists could not believe that he could calculate by how much the level of Lake Trasimeno (which depended almost entirely on rainfall) would rise during a period of rain so they laid a bet – the stately sum of 300 ducats. Don Benedetto won and true to his vow of poverty, handed over the money to the order.

It was here in the 18th century that the first ever scientific study of earthquakes began. It seems normal now, but in those days it was a dramatic break with tradition, and particularly so for a priest. For people here, as everywhere else, had always assumed that earthquakes were a punishment by God for some wickedness, or alternatively, the work of the Devil. And since they were supposedly caused by supernatural powers no one tried to find out more about them. Following the disastrous 1751 earthquake, Father Andrea Bina – who also happened to be a professor of physics at the Studium Perusinum, later known as Perugia University – set about investigating them scientifically. He invented a seismograph which consisted of a rough-hewn stone, about the size, shape and colour of a doner kebab, hanging on a rope from the high vaulted ceiling of the basement. Attached to the bottom of the stone was an iron spike which, when the earth moved, traced lines in a tray of sand below. From his observations Don Andrea wrote the first ever scientific treatise on earthquakes. A successor invented the anemometer which measures the speed and direction of wind.

The present head of the observatory, Father Martino Siciliani, a small, vivacious, white-haired priest, has also invented something. He pulls a device out of his jacket pocket which looks very much like a Blackberry. It is an earthquake alarm, which tells him whenever the earth moves in Umbria. 'It went off once during a conference in Djakarta,' he said delightedly, waving it in the air. 'I told them, "this is how you can be warned of tsunamis".'

Umbria, he explains, is sitting on the great fault line between the Eurasian tectonic place and the North African plate. The line runs from Morocco and Tunisia to Sicily and up near the coast of Italy to Naples and on northwards through the Appenines before curving eastwards through Friuli into Yugoslavia and Greece. Umbria has suffered devastating major earthquakes, usually with long periods of calm in between, he says. But it is still vulnerable to smaller, local earthquakes which can be quite violent, but affect only limited areas.

It is still not possible to predict earthquakes, Father Martino says. They can, however, monitor the fore-shocks, and the changes in the temperature and chemical composition of the water in springs which indicate that one is coming. 'But it is never enough. We are not yet able to interpret the signs well enough.'

Nevertheless in the months leading up to the 1997 earthquake he contacted the prefect of Perugia and suggested she have tents sent up into the mountains where the epicentre was likely to be. She hesitated, but he assured her that even if there were no quake it would be a useful exercise and she agreed. Ten days later, on 26 September at 2.33 a.m. it came, at a force of 5.5 on the Richter scale. Nine hours after, at 11.40 a.m., came the second even stronger shock at 5.8. There was a further shock of between 4 and 5 on the following 20 October. The tents sent up to the Colfiorito area, Father Martino said, 'turned out to be very, very useful'.

Father Martino had studied very carefully Father Bina's description of the 1751 earthquake and realised that the one in 1997 was following a remarkably similar pattern. After the first shock, his instruments picked up many more at a rate of about 20 to 30 an hour, imperceptible to most of the public but a sign that, as in 1751, there would be a second, powerful quake. He warned journalists who called to tell everyone: 'Be prudent! If you can avoid it, don't go back into your houses!' Tragically a group of people, including a camera crew, followed conflicting advice from another seismologist in Rome and entered the Basilica of St. Francis at Assisi. Four of them were killed. It is no consolation that at the same time frescoed plaster crashing down from the roof in a cloud of dust and debris was caught on film.

The observatory, partly lined with books and yellowing periodicals, is spacious and quiet. A reconstruction of Don Andrea's first seismograph stands there, but the highly-sensitive devices that now scratch out lines on long strips of blackened paper are ultra modern. They are linked directly to the solid rock below the monastery and to computers. In case of a serious quake, an alarm sets off Father Martino's phone. At the same time a blue light, like those on police cars, starts flashing in the observatory and a printer instantly prints out the readings. The recording of the 1997 earthquake is pinned to the wall near it, a wild forest of jagged lines; they look like the crazed scribblings of a madman.

Father Bina's work and that of his Benedictine successors is little known. The writers of non-Italian encyclopaedias appear to be unaware of his invention and his treatise and attribute the first efforts in seismology to British, German or other scientists of the 19th century – over a hundred years later. Father Martino is neither surprised or upset. 'As a matter of principle we religious do not advertise ourselves. That's why a lot of people don't know about us.'

Money

Filippo Antonelli, who owns large and successful wine-growing estates both in Umbria and near Rome, tells how, when he was a boy, his grandmother used to lead the family's summer migration from Rome to their country home in Umbria. The journey was much slower in those days and they used to stop for a rest near Narni, at a pastry shop where a little old lady used to sell the most delicious biscuits.

On one such journey they stopped at the shop as usual, but to their dismay it no longer sold the biscuits. When asked why, the little old lady said, 'I've stopped making them. Everybody wanted them.'

It is not fair to say that this is a typical example of Umbrian business attitudes, but the region is not exactly famous for its entrepreneurial genius either. There are a few great exceptions: Giorgio Lungarotti who in the 1960s pioneered quality wine at Torgiano, near Perugia, and built up a large and greatly-respected wine firm. Marco Caprai of Montefalco who developed and marketed Sagrantino wine and made it one of the most sought-after wines on the international market. And there is Mario Arcangeli, founder of the internationally-famous furnishing textiles firm Mastro Raphael which grew out of the Umbrian handweaving tradition. Tucked away in the little town of Massa Martana is Angelantoni, a world-level firm specialising in advanced refrigeration technology for a large variety of scientific purposes and which supplies equipment for NASA's space research in America.

In 1827 a woman in Borgo San Sepolchro, just over the border in Tuscany, unlike the old lady in the Narni pastry shop, realised she could make money from her remarkable skills in making pasta. So Giulia Buitoni sold her jewellery, set up a small workshop and founded what became a huge international firm based in Perugia. A descendant co-founded the chocolate firm Perugina, which for St Valentine's day in 1922, launched the 'Baci' (kisses) chocolates which became world-famous. But both Buitoni and Perugina ran into difficulties in the 1980s and ended up in the hands of Nestlé.

Apart from the industries around Terni, which were brought from outside Umbria, the Industrial Revolution passed Umbria by. Clerical rule provided poor incentives for enterprise and landlocked Umbria had long since dwindled into a backwater far from the main roads and rail lines. Umbrian firms, mostly founded since the Second World War, are usually small and often owned and run by members of one family. At the same time more than 6 per cent of the population are public employees, a staggering figure and the highest of any Italian region, and although Umbria is far more affluent than it was a generation ago, it is still dependent on additional funds from the national government. Alone, it could not pay these employees salaries or afford the health, social services and other amenities it enjoys today.

'Thousands of millions of individuals are working, producing and saving, in spite of everything we can think up in order to harass, obstruct and discourage them. They are driven not only by thirst for money but by a natural vocation. The pleasure and pride in seeing their own firms prosper, gaining a reputation, inspiring trust in ever-increasing numbers of customers, expanding their establishments and embellishing their offices is as powerful a spur to progress as is (the striving for) profit. If it were not so, one could not explain why there are entrepreneurs who lavish their energies and invest all their capital in their firm only to get returns which are far more modest than what they would comfortably and reliably earn in other employment.' These remarks by a former President of Italy, the economist Luigi Einaudi, hang on the wall in the offices of a firm which produces hand-made terracotta tiles in Castel Viscardi, not far from Orvieto. They certainly could explain the dedication of the artist who lovingly paints Renaissance arabesques onto Deruta plates and vases, or the craftsman who cuts, polishes and pieces together *intarsio* marquetry such as adorn the choir stalls of the Basilica at Assisi and other great churches, or who weave linen cloths with designs that passed down from the Middle Ages.

It is true that the politicians have made life hard for these ancient crafts, imposing taxes and regulations which, for instance, make it difficult to take on apprentices who will one day carry on the trade. Mounting costs and changing fashions have also played a part. Some have disappeared completely. The wonderful wrought ironwork one sees in the streets of Assisi would indicate that here there are superb blacksmiths, but when I telephoned the local Chamber of Commerce a few years ago to find their names and addresses I was told, 'so sorry *Signora*, the last one in town shut up shop for good two months ago'.

But plenty of others are still going strong, thanks not least to the tourist trade. Deruta is brimming over with hand-painted ceramics. There is everything from highly sophisticated and very expensive designs to crude and cheap versions of the traditional patterns. Many of the classical Deruta designs have been inspired by Perugino and other Umbrian Renaissance painters. Any attempt to look at the wares in even half the ceramics shops can leave one cross-eyed and totally bewildered. It is not a bad idea to go away and have a good night's sleep before deciding which object to buy.

Close to Deruta is Ripabianca which produces the clay and terracotta base for the ceramics. It also produces terracotta which is not for glazing and here firms sell handmade vases, plantpots, lamps and garden ornaments in every conceivable shape and size, and considerably cheaper than in any garden centre. This, like all the rest of Umbrian terracotta, is slightly rough and a peachy colour which is much softer and – to me – more attractive that the hard orange colour of Tuscan terracotta. Here, as with most Umbrian craftsmen, if you do not find what you are looking for, they will happily make things to your specifications and ship them to you at home.

In the Metropolitan Museum in New York is the famous 'studiolo' made in the 15th century for the palace of Duke Federico di Montefeltro in Gubbio. It consists of a small room made up of *trompe l'oeuil* intarsio panels which create the illusion of half-open cupboards with beautiful objects inside: musical and scientific instruments, insignia, armour. It was made in Gubbio itself and is the height of Renaissance craftsmanship. Craftsmen still make this kind of intarsio work in Gubbio, Città di Castello and Todi, although their products nowadays tend to be much less ambitious. They also made musical instruments – violins, cellos, lutes – and, particularly in Città di Castello, reproduction furniture. There are firms in Città di Castello, for instance, which make only chairs in every conceivable design. I once went there to buy some and in the end had to go home again and return another day, so vast and bewildering was the choice.

A regime?

We were forming an association of citizens to try and save what remained of the countryside around our town, a sizeable part of which had already been disfigured by squalid factories, warehouses and vast concrete parking lots. Amid much argument we had laboriously worked out the statute and we were about to draw up a list of founder members. Shall we put down the names of everyone present? Many hands went not up, but forward, in the Italian gesture of warding off the unwanted: 'not me!', 'not me!'

We all knew that the town council would instinctively see our association as a hotbed of political opposition. It definitely was not, but we knew their mentality. The refusals came from professional people, particularly architects, who had to deal almost daily with local politicians or officials, and from people who needed the council's support for certain projects of their own. But there were also people, such as housewives, who had nothing whatever to lose and yet were still afraid to expose themselves, no matter how much they sympathised with the cause.

I was among those who put their names forward. An hour or so later – the word having got around town fast as usual – my architect rang up and said, 'Do you think it is wise to expose yourself like that? Just when you have applied to the *comune* for permission to make alterations to your house?' I said that it was a risk I was prepared to take. (As it happened, permission was granted without any problems.)

I have no idea if this reluctance to stand up to authority is a legacy of centuries under the papacy, or the 20 years under Fascism or what. But I should add that the refusals were in a way the more militant ones, for several others had already declined to take part in the association at all, saying, 'it's useless, you will never get anywhere.' And we had heard members of groups like us fighting environmental issues in other *comuni* complain again and again, 'it's like beating your head against a rubber wall'.

Do we in Umbria live under a regime? Umbrian intellectuals like to debate this at length. Even the saintly archbishop of Perugia, Monsignor Giuseppe Chiaretti has called it a regime and provoked a peeved retort from the region's prime minister. Of course, Umbria is no North Korea or Iran. Umbrians are as free as everyone else in Italy to boot out their town, provincial and regional administrations when elections come around. The only difference is that they don't. For the past 60 years, with rare exceptions, they have regularly returned the same party to power in the towns, in the two provinces and (since it was established in 1972) the regional government. This party was once known as the Communists, it is now called the Democratic Party, and it governs usually with other left-wing allies.

It is not that the majority of Umbrians are dyed-in-the-wool Reds. During the previous two decades, Umbria had been one of the most staunchly Fascist regions in the country, but most of them were not extreme right-wingers either. They were just susceptible to anyone who wooed poor farmers, made them feel wanted, gave them a sense of dignity. Then came the war and disillusionment, and in the 1948 elections, the first after the war, Umbrians did a 190-degree turn and voted for the Communists who also claimed to be on their side and promised to end their poverty. Thus Umbria became, with Tuscany and Emilia-Romagna, part of the 'red belt' stretching across the middle of Italy; and unlike its two bigger and more developed neighbours, it remained thus.

There is no doubt about it, under the Left Umbria has moved from bitter poverty to the relative affluence of today. How much of this was due to the general transformation of Italy and how much to efforts of the region's politics is hard to say. But in the meanwhile those in power have been weaving a vast web to keep themselves there. Following the pattern of their Fascist predecessors they set up a myriad of public or semi-public bodies to take care of almost every imaginable side of life, from farmers' cooperatives to historical think-tanks, whose staff owe them their jobs. Then there are many hundreds more employed in the town, provincial and regional bureaucracies and their services, and an untold number of consultants, businessmen and building firms who depend on official permits and government contracts. Whatever their personal political views, all these people and their families have every interest in voting the PD or their allies back into power each time.

'It is no mystery to anyone,' said one of the most authoritative experts on Umbria and political parties, Professor Ernesto Galli della Loggia, 'that ... six months before the elections the offices of the Regional government, the town councils and their various departments suddenly empty and all who work there – and most of them are members of the PD – leave their desks and go around, house by house, campaigning, promising things, reminding people of things and sometimes even intimidating people and threatening them. This is what keeps the electorate tied to those who govern.'

The right-wing opposition parties, in many places, seem unable to present a credible alternative. I have met no one who seriously thinks that, barring some major political earthquake like the massive corruption scandals which toppled the long-entrenched centre-left national regime in Rome in the 1990s, things will ever change. Although it is widely assumed that there is corruption in some form or another it rarely comes to light. The PD bears little resemblance to the Communist Party of the old days; the few remaining convinced Communists have taken refuge in little splinter parties. It seems interested more in retaining power rather than creating a better future. There is no lack of good intentions, but these tend to remain empty declarations while things go on the same as ever.

The Catholic Church, which used to own Umbria and which long wielded a powerful influence in Italian politics, holds little sway in the Umbria of today. For all their saints and martyrs, their churches, monasteries and religious orders, Umbrians are no more religious than their contemporaries elsewhere. Vocations are declining, the lists of parish priests contain numerous foreign names – without imported priests from Poland or Africa one suspects that many ancient parishes would have to close. Freemasonry, a reaction to clerical rule in Umbria, is still active and attracts members from across the political spectrum. The ruling PD, although not actively anti-clerical, is by definition a secular party. The Archbishop of Perugia summed up the political situation in 2006: 'In Umbria we have been in difficulties for 60 years; there is a widespread weariness, also among Catholics, caused by these years of "regime", which has given rise to a disaffection with politics. We urgently need to become committed again.'

During the brouhaha which followed his remarks, the Archbishop explained that by 'regime' he meant the 'persistence in power' and complained that it was 'demotivating' the Catholic laity. 'There is no longer the habit of debate nor the desire to get involved because it seems that nothing can ever change.' The Catholic influence is absent from the Umbrian cultural scene, from its politics and its media, he lamented.

The controversy raging in our town illustrates in miniature some of the problems facing Umbria today.

Our *comune* comprises a lovely old hill town, beautiful olive-covered hillsides and an area of flatter land in the valley. The town belongs to a variety of conservation associations and the town council has long been declaring its commitment to protect the environment. But many inhabitants have watched with growing concern as the land in the valley became increasingly covered by small factories, warehouses, workshops and concrete spaces packed with new or used cars, agricultural machinery and concrete fireplaces. New industrial areas are for ever being opened, even though a considerable number of old factories or warehouses lie empty, their occupants usually having gone out of business. No one is against industries as such, but all deplore their mindless spread, their ugliness and the lack of any effort to blend them in with the environment.

We were finally galvanised into forming an association and taking action by the town council approving a plan to build a huge 'tourist village' on some of the remaining land in the valley. On the face of it there would seem to be nothing wrong with a tourist village in a region which is trying to attract more tourism. But this village was to consist of 60,000 cubic metres of buildings, including a hotel and a hundred separate houses, each divided into two apartments. It was of the size and style one would expect in an Adriatic seaside resort, not in an Umbrian valley.

But what really set alarm bells ringing was the fact that this supposedly five-star 'village' would be situated immediately next to a busy, noisy main road and flanked on three sides by industries, including two chemical works. What tourists would come to Umbria and pay good money to stay there? The constructor and the mayor insisted that many people from all over the world would come but were not convincing. Even more worryingly, neither could say what would become of the buildings when, as seemed guaranteed, the 'tourist' project failed.

It seemed quite obvious: it was a transparent attempt at building speculation. Thanks to dubious manoeuvrings and loopholes in the regulations, which allowed 'tourist' building where 'residential' building was forbidden, what had once been zoned as agricultural land could now be built on. The town's population did not need any new housing, the buildings were evidently intended for inhabitants of a larger town nearby looking for cheaper homes, and thus we risked becoming simply a dormitory for the town next door.

Interestingly, the constructor told us it was people in or close to the town council who had proposed the idea. Equally interestingly, he said he took the members of the right-wing opposition out to dinner and persuaded them of the excellence of his project. What else may have passed between any of these we do not know. The fact remains that the only person who voted against the plan was the councillor responsible for the environment, who happened to belong to one of the Communist splinter parties. He immediately came under massive pressure to resign, which he resisted, and has been ostracised by the rest of the administration.

The town council continued to defend the project tooth and nail, and at the time of writing the outcome was uncertain. As one of our group remarked, we seemed to have taken on the role of a small stone which has been dropped into a piece of well-oiled machinery, in which two elements which should be separate and independent work together closely for the profit of both.

Food

'Umbrian cooking,' says Sonia Chellini, the president of the Umbrian branch of Slow Food, 'is very simple, one could say very Franciscan, because it was the cooking of the poor.' There are very few elaborate dishes such as rich people would have had their servants make. 'But' she adds, 'the ingredients are fantastic.' Slow Food, which was founded in Italy but has spread world-wide, fights to save local products and specialities. Signora Chellini and her colleagues have already rescued some excellent Umbrian products from oblivion and are working to save several more.

There is no better way of appreciating the food one has at home in Umbria than walking into some chic delicatessen in London. There the virgin olive oil sold in precious little bottles costs the earth. It is usually not as good, and many times more expensive than what I buy when I take my oil canisters along to my neighbours Fabio and Rita after the olive harvest. I watch the green-gold liquid flowing from their big containers in their storeroom into my smaller one, knowing that they would never dream of using any artificial fertilisers or pesticides on their olive trees. The new oil is special – for the first month or so after pressing it tastes strong and peppery and Umbrians spread it alone on bread or *bruschetta* just to savour the taste.

On fine days in the autumn my doctor's surgery is deserted. All the grandmas and grandpas who normally fill the waiting room, quietly mulling over their aches and pains, are up ladders in the olive trees, combing the olives with plastic combs into sacks tied round their waists, which are wired at the rim to stay open. A stream of cheerful village gossip spills from the trees like a song from a lark. Their way of picking olives, if ever they were to work it out, is very expensive – although many people I know keep most of it for themselves or to pass on to friends and relations. Which is why instead of chatter you may hear strange noises coming from other olive groves. Weird machines brush or blow olives into containers, sometimes from trees curiously pruned into the shape of fir trees. Even weirder ones have dragons' wings that embrace the tree like an upturned umbrella and shake it vigorously so the olives fall into its folds. In terms of costs, such machines beat the grandma-and-grandpa method hands down, but many of the olive groves are too small, too steep or too irregularly-planted for modern methods. Umbrian oil, although excellent, tends to be far from lucrative.

More pound notes flutter on to delicatessen counters for the dainty little jars of capers and caper apples with cute little tags, whereas here, if you get your timing right and the neighbours don't get there first, you can simply pick them from the plants that grow everywhere on the limestone walls. You can even grow them on your own garden wall – at least in theory. Capers are very self-willed and tend to grow where *they* want, not where *you* want. I have tried buying them at garden centres but none ever took. It is said that the seeds are spread by lizards who like to eat the caper fruit, and eliminate the seeds in their faeces as they dart around the walls. Locals say one method of getting capers to grow is to mix the seeds with soil and press it all deep into cracks in the rock. Others believe in blowing them in to cracks sharply through a straw. The previous owner of my house, Giancarlo, claims he planted the two caper plants that grow on my garden wall by artificially reproducing the lizards' method. He took the seeds from the fruit and soaked them in water. The ones that floated, which were presumably empty and no good, he threw away. The heavier ones that sank he rubbed together with sand so as to scratch the skin of the seeds, then mixed the seeds and sand with manure and stuffed it into the cracks in the wall. Apparently it worked.

I can't say I preserve capers because the flowers, when allowed to come out, are so exotic and beautiful, large and white with a spray of purple-tipped stamens, that I cannot bear to pick the tight little buds (which is what capers are). I have not yet seriously tried to bottle the fruit.

If capers are recalcitrant, truffles are much, much worse. They grow in various forests in Umbria and are an important part of Umbrian cuisine, as well as a valuable export. One is not allowed to search for them without a licence. You can buy saplings here with truffle-bearing roots to plant. But take them home and plant them in your garden and the chances of them ever producing anything are about as great as you getting to the moon. Unless the humus, the position and the climate are absolutely right, no truffle is ever going to consider developing, and basically they only ever consent to grow where truffles have always grown before.

Until recently it was generally considered impossible to cultivate truffles; they are collected by truffle hunters who go out into woods with special long-handled diggers with a small sharp blade on the end and their trained truffle dogs. (Pigs are not normally used in Umbria, not least because they reputedly try to eat what they find.) The truffles they find – the number and quality vary from year to year – are passed on to to one middleman, then another, then an exporter and so on until they end up on the counters of Fortnum and Masons costing the earth.

In the past Umbrians never bothered much about truffles. Only occasionally would someone go out and search for some to sell to gourmets in the bigger cities, they did not eat them themselves. Or more precisely, according to Sergio Consoli, who is Slow Food's Umbrian truffle expert, they ate the first truffles of the winter, not the delicious ones that come later but big dark lumps which they would boil and eat like potatoes. These did not taste of anything in particular, they simply filled the stomach. It was only after the Second World War, as people became more affluent and tourism took off that they became aware what black, and sometimes white, gold lay hidden in their woods.

Even now, truffles are not usually given the star treatment they get in foreign gourmet shops. When in season they simply get lined up alongside mozzarella, sun-dried tomatoes and artichoke hearts on the cheese-and-salami counters of grocers' shops. Even simple restaurants offer pasta, risottos, scrambled eggs or meat done with truffles – black ones that is. The white ones are much rarer, ten times more expensive and are usually whisked off to some lucrative foreign market before one can even set eyes on them – indeed I have never yet seen a white Umbrian truffle. There are several varieties of the black ones but for normal purposes they are divided into summer truffles, which are lighter in taste and cheaper, and winter truffles which come at the beginning of winter, have a more intense taste and cost more. Even here the price for either kind might seem daunting – at the time of writing, black ones cost around 500 Euros a kilogramme and white ones between 5,000 and 6,000 Euros – but truffles are very light and a little goes a long way. Signor Consoli taught me that they will last a month or so if wrapped carefully in absorbent paper, such as kitchen paper, placed in a small, tightly closed jam jar and kept as much as possible in the fridge. Packed that way they can easily survive a car trip back home. The absorbent paper is important because it keeps them dry: humidity causes them to go mouldy. Before cooking the rough dark outer skin should be scraped off. Black truffles taste a lot better if warmed in butter or oil first. White truffles should be served raw. I prefer to buy them from specialised truffle and *funghi* shops because there they are likely to be fresher. One should look very carefully at truffle sauces, conserved truffles and truffle oil before buying. Truffle sauces labelled *Salsa di Tartufi* should be all right, *Salsa Tartu-fata* is usually bits of truffle mixed with other things – usually black olives and still quite tasty – and the *Salsa al Sapore di Tartufi* or oil of a similar description is best left alone. The Umbrian truffle world has not been without its scandals – several people were once arrested when it was found that dealers had been buying tasteless truf-fles from abroad and injecting them with truffle-tasting liquid. Worse still, someone discovered that methane gas can smell like truffles, piped it into olive oil and sold it as truffle oil.

Once I thought of training my cocker spaniel, Sasha, to hunt truffles. Sasha had a great nose. He could smell a crumb of pizza in the gutter at a good 50 metres and it seemed a good idea to turn his talent to some more useful purpose. I fancied giving dinner parties when I would say nonchalantly 'oh, the truffles ... I found them myself.' I asked around until I found someone who trained truffle dogs. 'You have to start when they are puppies,' he told me. 'You take a small piece of truffle and wind wool or cotton thread around it until you have a ball. Then you and the puppy play ball with it so the puppy associates the smell with pleasant experiences.' That, plus rewards, gives the dog the incentive to seek them out in the forest. Alas, by then Sasha was well into middle age and set in his ways and so I had to abandon the idea.

Truffles, even white ones, are not the most expen-sive product in Umbria. That record is held by saffron. Within the space of less than a decade saffron has shot like a meteor from complete oblivion to its position as one of the stars of Umbrian cuisine. During the Middle Ages and Renaissance, much used to be grown in the valleys below the Appenines. Records show that it was greatly coveted, often used for payment instead of money, sometimes stolen and subject to strict laws. It was used not only as a spice but also as a dye and Perugino – who came from Città della Pieve where much was produced – used it in his paints. But then it seemed to fall out of fashion and after about the 16th century no one bothered growing it any more. Then suddenly at the beginning of this century it was back again, around Citta della Pieve, Cascia and a couple of smaller areas.

Each has its own story. In Cascia a study by anthropologists from the University of Perugia into the medieval saffron industry sparked the idea of trying it again. Following old documents describing how it was done in the Middle Ages, the first few bulbs of purple-flowered *crocus sativus*, the saffron crocus, were planted experimentally in 1998. By 2006, twenty-eight farmers were growing it and a total of 5,000 square metres were under cultivation. An association was formed and modern marketing methods adopted. Gianluca Polidori, the association's president, puts its success down to a growing demand for genuine, biological foods and also a trend to more sophisticated cooking. Gourmet restaurants are among their best customers. But also, he says, because of its medicinal properties. 'It is known to be an antioxidant, it combats aging. In England it also used to be used as an antidepressant. It makes one feel better.' Was there any basis for its long-standing reputation as an aphrodisiac? I wanted to know.

'I don't think that has been investigated scientifically, but it is known to have a positive effect on the female hormones,' he said.

The saffron crocuses flower in the autumn and on St Catherine's day, 25th November. The Cascia producers meet to set that year's minimum price. In 2006, it was 24 Euros a gramme. But if you bought their saffron in a fancy gourmet shop rather than from the producer it could have cost you as much as 40 Euros a gramme. You could console yourself however with the knowledge that one gramme will make about 40 servings of *risotto allo zafferano.*

To appreciate why it costs so much one might go and stay in an *agriturismo* run by one of the Cascia saffron farmers in October and watch. They go out before dawn and pick the flowers before the sun comes up and the petals open – the taste is best that way. The same evening everyone sits round the fire and pulls each single flower apart very gently and extracts the three red stigma which are then dried, sometimes over glowing charcoal. According to some estimates it takes 150,000 flowers to produce a kilogramme of saffron, others say 200,000. The 2006 production around Cascia was four kilos. Umbrian saffron is more expensive than that produced in much larger quantities in Iran and other Asian countries but, producers here suggest, it tastes better.

The woods and fields here yield up many more treasures, if one only knows where to look. Not only mushrooms of many types – again one needs a licence – but all sorts of delicious vegetables which rarely find their way into the shops.

One can still see old ladies with headscarves and plastic bags in the fields and olive groves bent over, picking things. It is they who know where to find *rapunzoli*, tiny plants with delicious little roots, *strigoli* which look rather like couch grass and taste like wild asparagus, or *cicorietta*, the bitter wild chicory which tastes delicious when blanched, then sautéed with garlic and a little hot pepper in olive oil. Sometimes they come away with wild fennel, thyme and mint, or bunches of borage, not to put in vases despite its pretty blue flowers, but to cook or eat raw in salads. Their children and grandchildren do not have time for such pastimes, so the number of people who know what to look for and where are fewer and fewer, and this wonderful produce ever rarer. One can find them occasionally in some restaurants with good contacts to those marvellous old ladies, or on a market stall, but it is a matter of luck.

There are many more bent figures to be seen around the countryside in spring when the wild asparagus starts growing. Many people go out and gather the thin, very dark green and strong-tasting shoots of wild asparagus, rather than pay the astronomic prices that it fetches in the shops. There is a special tool for this too: a stick with tongs at the end which enables one to pick the stalks without getting one's arms shredded by the prickly branches of the old plants and without having too close an encounter with any snake that might be lurking there. Cooked, it is delicious in risottos, pasta dishes or as an accompaniment to fried eggs.

Slow Food arrived in Umbria just in time. It has saved the delicious *fagiolino del Trasimeno*, a tiny bean with a delicate taste which grows, as the name suggests, around Lake Trasimeno. The locals call the beans *risina* – little rice – because they are so small. They are believed to have been imported from Africa in ancient times, and had survived only in the vegetable patches of one or two fans before they were rescued. They are still not easy to find outside the area but one can buy them from the better grocers' shops around the lake. Because their taste is very subtle they should not be cooked, as beans often are, with ham or sausages but simply boiled and served with olive oil, salt and pepper as a side dish.

Slow Food conducted a similar campaign to re-launch the excellent fish of Lake Trasimeno and with it the livelihood of the fishermen who were gradually abandoning their boats and are now thriving again. Further afield they have worked to save the Cannara onion from oblivion. This small, flat, golden and very sweet onion was in danger of being cross-bred with more common varieties until it was no longer recognisable.

The next on the list for Slow Food was the 'black celery' of Trevi, near Foligno. It is actually not black, but green like normal celery, although it is said to go dark if it is allowed to revert to the wild state. It is a special variety of celery which looks very much like the usual kind except it is bigger and tastes more intense and much, much better. If it grew in France it would doubtless be famous and sought after by top chefs. But production is very limited and for the most part it is consumed locally. The celery is eaten with oil and salt, or stuffed with minced meat, tomato and parmesan and served with a tomato sauce.

As we spoke, Signora Chellini also had her sights on Umbrian chickpeas, wild peas and the sheep's cheese of the Valnerina.

Black celery is the speciality in the 'taverne' during Trevi's month-long festivities in October, which is just the time the celery is at its best. The 'taverne' are rustic eateries with trestle tables in vaulted cellars and are the cold-weather version of the open air ones in squares or fields in the summer and they function in the same way. This is the best opportunity of all to enjoy traditional Umbrian food and wines in their natural setting. The housewives back in the kitchen – good, traditional cooks who produce ancient dishes their mothers and grand-mothers cooked before them – are often called on to whip up large dinners for friends' weddings, baptisms or confirmation celebrations but they would never have considered themselves anything special. But Signora Chellini and Slow Food have started an organisation of these women, calling them *cuoche popolare* – folk cooks – and encouraging them to pass on traditional recipes and skills to the next generation.

The great gastronomic centre of Umbria is Norcia. When I first drove to Norcia, many years ago, and looked down from the road into the lush upland valley where the town nestles, my first reaction was: 'this must be the Land of Cockayne!' And indeed it is, as was confirmed shortly afterwards by a stroll through the town with its food shops packed with hams, sausages, cheeses, truffles and sacks upon sacks of lentils, beans, spelt and other good things.

It is Norcia's good fortune, firstly to be in the middle of a mountain plateau with very fertile soil, but also to be blessed with rare '*marcite*'. These are warm springs whose temperature is said to remain constant at around 11°, winter and summer alike. In the Middle Ages, maybe even as far back as the 5th or 6th century AD, Benedictine monks diverted these into myriad little channels which irrigate a wide area, producing grass which is a vivid green all the year round and is so fast-growing that it can be mown for hay ten to a dozen times a year.

Of course the modern world is encroaching in Umbria too. Cheap battery chickens, ready-to-cook suppers and splendid-looking but tasteless apples fill the supermarket shelves. In country areas markets tend to be disappointing, mostly consisting of stalls with cheap clothes and shoes and few of the fresh farm goods one would expect – mainly because most people have their own fruit trees and vegetable patches. But with a little determination one can still buy home-made *pecorino*, sheep's cheese, from the shepherd, olive oil from the grower, and sausage straight from the producer. And indeed, as Signora Chellini points out, the greatest incentive to cultivate Umbria's wonderful products and cooking traditions is the presence of tourists who so greatly enjoy them.

At table

Sooner or later one ends up in a restaurant and the first thing that arrives on the table is, inevitably, the bread. Oh dear. For many this can be a bad start; the bread is saltless. Umbria's unsalted bread has been blamed on Pope Paul III and his salt tax which prompted the unsuccessful 'salt war'. This may be so, although bread is saltless in other parts of Italy where the Popes did not rule. Presumably the Umbrians got to like it so that even when salt became cheap bread remained unsalted. Foreign visitors tend to find it pretty unappetising but it is not wise to say so, people here can get quite defensive about it. You will be told that it makes a good accompaniment to the spicy salamis and hams of the region, and indeed when it is very fresh and well-made it can be quite pleasant. When Giancarlo Menotti was starting the Festival of the Two Worlds in Spoleto, he tried to persuade bakers to make salted bread, at least for the duration of the summer festival, which in the end they did, but reverted to the traditional kind when it was over. As people became more nutrition conscious, bakers started baking wholemeal bread, but it was still unsalted and in my view even less appetising than the white. In recent years however bakers have started selling *ciabatta* and Roman or Apulian types of bread which are salted and definitely tastier.

A real Umbrian bread that tastes good is the *Torta al*

Testo, a flat bread said to be Etruscan in origin. It is made with flour, oil and salt, rolled out and cut into rounds like pizzas. It is then baked on the *testo* which is a flat stone or plate of terracotta placed on the embers of the fire. It is cut open like pitta bread and ham, cooked sausages and sauteed greens are put inside.

Large dishes of antipasto may arrive on the table, often with *crostini* or *bruschetta* (both roasted slices of bread) with chicken liver, olive, truffle or some other sauce on them, slices of ham, cheese and salami and maybe a little truffle omelette. If done well with fresh truffles this can be absolutely delicious.

Somewhat tastier than ordinary bread is a yellowish cheesy bread which is often served with antipasto. This is a relative of the traditional Easter speciality, *Pizza di Pasqua*, which is not flat like normal pizzas but more like a tall sponge cake and is made of flour, cheese, lard and large quantities of eggs. There is also a sweet version. Soon after I arrived, I asked my favourite grocer if he sold free-range eggs as well as the battery eggs on display. 'No *Signora*,' was his reply. 'We are not allowed to sell good things like that.' Then dropping his voice to a whisper he added 'but if you ask the lady at the cash desk, she'll be able to help you'. And indeed, hidden away in a large brown paper bag, in defiance of all the regulations, were fresh farm eggs brought by some farmer's wife that morning. How many did I want? So I happily went on buying her under-the-counter fresh eggs until one spring day there was not a single one to be had. 'Sorry,' said the lady at the cash desk 'but everybody is making their *Pizze di Pasqua*.'

No matter how good the antipasto, it is wise to leave plenty of room for the pasta which could well be *strangozzi*. Slightly rough, made just with flour and water and thicker than spaghetti, they are also known as *strozzapreti* or *strangulapreti*, all names that seem to betray a burning desire to throttle priests, which after centuries of heavy-handed rule by the Church seems to have been shared by quite a number of Umbrians. In fact, one impeccable source claims the name was inspired by the short ropes that anti-clericals would have ready as they waited behind dark corners at night for some unfortunate priest to come by. The best, most Umbrian way of eating them is with truffles, and one must hope that the cook is generous with the grater. But they are good with all sorts of sauces.

Spring is the time for the delicious *frittata* or scrambled eggs with wild asparagus, and winter the best time for *frittata* with truffles, although many places serve it all the year round. A very Umbrian dish is *zuppa di farro*, a thick and filling soup made of spelt grains and vegetables. Now that farro is so fashionable, more imaginative cooks have invented all sorts of new dishes around it. The more queasy might want to steer clear of *paiata* or *pagliata* which is chopped-up entrails, usually of chicken. People say it is very good but I have never been tempted to try it.

Meat dishes do not rank high in the Umbrian cuisine, probably because ordinary people were not often able to afford meat and when they could, it was simple cuts that they would roast or grill over an open fire. And in fact grilled ribs of lamb tend to be very good. Grilled sausages, if made by hand locally, are even better. Of the stews, the tastiest in my opinion is *tagliata all'aceto balsamico* which is sliced beef cooked in balsamic vinegar.

Umbrian desserts are unlikely to win any prizes for *haute patisserie*, being rustic, rather heavy and usually variations of pastry, raisins, nuts, spices and dried fruits, often laced with a sticky red liqueur called *alchermes*. Pleasant exceptions are *brutti ma buoni* – literally 'ugly but good' – which are small, light almond pastries, excellent when fresh; and *tozzetti*, a harder, crunchier almond pastry, the equivalent to Tuscany's *cantuccini*, which you dip in liquorous *Vin Santo*, or better still, in the sweet *passito di Sagrantino* from the Montefalco area.

Italy's Burgundy

Giampaolo Tabarrini's maternal grandfather used to feed his oxen two and a half litres of wine each and every morning before taking them out to plough. The wine gave them extra energy, his grandson says, and apparently they still managed to plough a straight furrow.

Tabarrini's grandfather would have seriously doubted the sanity of anyone who told him that the wine grown in the vineyards around his home down of Montefalco would ever be worth much more than that, much less become world famous, or that this area of Umbria could ever be called Italy's Burgundy. For his was the Umbrian peasant's view of wine, a foodstuff like milk and bread which gave them energy, and above all to be grown cheaply in large quantities and sold quickly before it could mature. Much of it was exported to be blended with French wines. Wine for them was not something that enhanced life, that one could savour at leisure and enjoy. Many centuries before, Umbrian wines must have been better. Pliny the Elder had good words to say about a variety called Itriola which grew around Montefalco, and which people think might have been what is now called Sagrantino. It seems to have been appreciated in the Renaissance; the painters Perugino and Pinturicchio asked to be paid partly in wine, but with the rare exceptions (there are always a few exceptions to everything in

Umbria), since anyone could remember in much of the region they were very ordinary. So much so that Orvieto, whose white wines had been famous for centuries, even once tried to persuade the public that although the town lay in Umbria, its wines were to be considered Tuscan!

Under the system of sharecropping, which survived in Umbria right into the 1950s, no one had any particular interest in investing money and effort into improving the quality of their wine. Later the formation of cooperatives and the collective marketing of wine, dear to the Communist administration, had a similar effect. It was only in the 1960s that one man, Giorgio Lungarotti, an agronomist, firmly broke with tradition. Deeply influenced by winegrowing in France, he turned his land around Torgiano, close to Perugia, into specialised vineyards, with high-quality vines and and new, sophisticated methods of production. Two of his first wines, the white Torre di Giano and the red Rubesco, are now Umbrian classics, but when they first came out they represented a historic breakthrough – wines for a new kind of lifestyle, wines of quality to be appreciated, not just quaffed. Not satisfied with that, Lungarotti began to aim for the equivalent of the French grand cru and produced, among his other wines, the Torgiano Rosso Riserva which is now one of the 30 or so Italian top wines which bear the coveted DOCG* appellation.

Another blow to the old system was struck in 1986 when the Italian wine-poisoning scandal broke. Over

---

* denominatione d'origine controllata e garantita.

twenty people died, dozens were blinded and hundreds hospitalised after drinking cheap wine to which producers had added methyl alcohol, normally used as a paint solvent, to increase the alcohol content. Italy's wine exports plummeted, and the reputation of its wines, such as it was, was destroyed. The scandal shocked the Italian wine world into sweeping reforms – better controls, better techniques – and the idea that quality, not quantity, could pay began to take hold.

In 1971 Arnaldo Caprai, a textile industrialist, bought vineyards and set up a winery in Montefalco. He had doubtless watched Lungarotti closely but he had another idea. Sagrantino was a vine which had long grown in this small area, some think it was the one mentioned by Pliny the Elder, others say it was brought by Franciscan monks from the Middle East. It was scarcely known outside the neighbourhood and wasn't even rated particularly highly by the locals. They used to make a sweet liquorous wine from it to drink with dessert with the family at Easter or Christmas festivals. This may be the origin of its name, or perhaps it was once used as Communion wine – there are various theories. The vines grew up the walls of houses or were strung between trees and many had been thrown out – in fact, it was threatened with extinction. But Arnaldo Caprai planted Sagrantino and used modern scientific techniques to develop it into a rich, full-bodied red wine. His second stroke of genius was to put his son Marco in charge of the business side of the winemaking. With the qualities of the wine and Marco's energy and skills in marketing, Sagrantino shot like a rocket in ten years from obscurity to a top place in the international hit parade. His success inspired others: dozens of producers in the area switched to Sagrantino and flew on his coattails to dizzy heights. Sagrantino, now also in the DOCG class, can be very expensive and, for many, reserved only for special occasions and special dishes. Rather than trying cheaper versions, which can occasionally be disappointing, it is better to try the Montefalco Rosso, an excellent DOC* wine produced by most vintners in the area and which must contain a certain percentage of Sagrantino, combined with more common varieties.

Thanks largely to Caprai, Sagrantino turned Montefalco into the perfect Umbrian success story: the ancient hilltop town that has been able to turn a traditional product into a major asset, thus preserving its beauty instead of resorting to environment-damaging industries. Tourists used to go to Montefalco to see the frescoes by Benozzo Gozzoli in the Museum of San Francesco and afterwards, in its restaurants and winebars, discover its excellent wines. Now they come for the wine and take in the frescoes while they are there. The winegrowers have developed a 'Strada del Sagrantino', a route through the pretty Sagrantino-growing area which combines wine and local cuisine with other lovely old towns like Bevagna and Giano and maybe ends with a visit to some winery and buying wine to take home. Even more fun is the wineries' open day, *cantine aperte*, in May. On payment of an

---

* A somewhat less stringent category, but still a greatly respected area appellation.

initial entrance fee, valid for all the wineries, one receives a glass and a kind of pocket to put it in and hang around one's neck while one tours the *cantine*, tasting the different wines. Those in the know head for the *cantine* which have lawns and trees to sit under. The traffic police are out in force, but only to keep the traffic moving through the country lanes; the alcohol content of the person behind the steering wheel does not appear to interest them.

Sitting in the sun outside a Montefalco or Bevagna wine bar sipping Sagrantino, or any other local wine, is one of the greatest Umbrian experiences. One would never guess the incredible amount of experimentation, scientific and marketing know-how, arguments, set-backs, paperwork and patience which went into this success, not to mention the unavoidable hard, physical work which has to be done now, as ever before, in the vineyards. 'I told Marco Caprai, "we should all put up a monument to your Dad, because he has given dignity to our hard work, which before him had no dignity and brought no glory"', Giampaolo Tabarrini said.

And success inspires more success: young Tabarrini, a ball of energy and enthusiasm, was experimenting light-heartedly with whites, almost as a joke, and produced an extraordinary white wine which already in its first year seemed destined to be another major success. He called it 'Ad Armando' after his other grandfather who taught him how to grow wine. The grape is a Trebbiano, but not the very common Italian Trebbiano whose strength is quantity rather than quality. It is Trebbiano Spoletino, which is very different even to look at, and like Sagrantino, is limited to this area. And Tabarrini's Trebbiano Spoletino is different from the rest because it comes from a part of the Tabarrini vineyards that somehow survived the great phylloxera plague that wiped out most of Europe's vines in the late 19th century. Thus the vines did not have the imported American root stock that was used to get European vineyards going again after the disaster and this may have influenced the character of the vines. As the first year's production of 3,000 bottles went on the market and was snapped up with in weeks, Tabarrini was keeping the whereabouts of these vines secret for fear people who try to take cuttings and damage them.

'Past reason hunted'

On a certain Sunday in September, most likely the third, a newcomer can wake up at dawn in horror, convinced that revolution has broken out. All over Umbria thousands upon thousands of men have got up in the dark, loaded guns and cases upon cases of ammunition into off-road vehicles, headed off into the countryside and started blasting away. Their targets are not politicians, though – some of the men *are* politicians – but wild birds and animals. The hunting season has begun. By the time it ends on 31 January countless thrushes, chaffinches, larks, hares, pheasants and other feathered and furry creatures, and quite likely a few human beings, will have lost their lives.

Hunting is of course an ancient and honourable activity, and for centuries in Umbria where every last chaffinch was desperately needed to help feed hungry families, it was a vital one. But that was then. Today 'hunting', as it is still called, bears little resemblance to what goes on under that name in other European countries and can sorely test a person's Umbriaphilia.

Thanks to ancient usage, later enshrined in a Fascist-era law, hunters have long been allowed to hunt over land not their own free of charge, whether the owners liked it or not – and so, with modifications, it remains today. The only sanctuaries are private gardens, parks, built-up areas and land surrounded by fences at least two and a half metres high – which makes it prohibitively expensive for people to fence off property of any size. 'Hunters' are not allowed to fire within a certain distance of houses and roads and never towards them, but this is widely ignored, as testified by friends who frequently have shot raining down on their roofs and coming in the windows.

Big landowners traditionally reserved the big game for themselves, so ordinary folk had to go after whatever small game they could find, like hares and little birds. As Italy grew affluent in the 1960s hundreds of thousands of novices, mostly town-dwellers, were able to sit the not-very-challenging exam for a hunting licence, buy guns, dress up like Rambo and start firing. Within a couple of decades, whole species had been exterminated and hunters who did not go out on the first days of the season would find few targets left.

It was partly thanks to pressure from indignant Germans, British and other European neighbours that carnage was eventually reduced somewhat, but also due to growing revulsion at home. Two referendums designed to stop hunters entering other people's property were held in 1990 and 1997. Both showed large majorities in favour but nevertheless were were declared invalid for lack of a quorum. But the results finally shocked politicians and the hunting lobby into reluctant action. The hunting season was drastically shortened – hunters claim it is now the shortest in Europe – and subjected to a variety of restrictions. (Among other things: hunting is forbidden on the territory of Assisi on 4 October, feast-day of St Francis, patron saint of birds and animals.) Hunters, farmers and environmentalists are obliged to work together to restore a balance between hunting and wildlife conservation. And – an important judicial and moral landmark – wild animals which hitherto had been legally regarded as belonging to no one, now belong to everyone – that is, the community.

But the battle continues. In Umbria, perhaps because there are more 'hunters' in proportion to the population than any other region, it arouses intense passions and controversies. One regional government fell in a dispute over hunting. Others have been passing bills concerning hunting at the rate, environmentalists have calculated, of one every four months. Even though hunters now make up only 5 per cent of the population and have a bad image, their organisation, the Federcaccia, still wields disproportionate power and influence. One would think, for instance, that the Regional Park of Lake Trasimeno would include the surrounding hillsides which drain into the lake. No, it consists only of the water itself, the sedge around it and a couple of small bits of the banks. This is the result of massive pressure from hunters while the Park was being created, which became so heated that Park officials got tomatoes thrown at them. Fortunately there are strict environmental rules covering the surrounding area.

The official, acceptable, face of hunting is presented by people like Alessandro Barbino, the president of its Perugia provincial branch. Barbino regularly sets out before dawn with one of his dogs looking for woodcock. He learned to love hunting as a boy when he would go out with his father. His father taught him where wood-cock and other birds are likely to nest, and how to use dogs to find them and raise them. When Barbino talks of the thrill of hunting, of the skill involved in training and working with dogs, in knowing where to go and in preparing hides, his enthusiasm is infectious and when he says that for true hunters the actual killing of the creature is not the most important thing, one can almost believe him. He does admit, regretfully, that there are 'abuses' – 'it's just a few people who give hunters a bad name,' he says. He insists that most hunters have become more responsible and more environmentally aware in recent years. They have repopulated the countryside, reintroducing species which had been wiped out. Umbrian hunters, moreover, do not indulge in the illegal trapping, netting and shooting of migratory birds which has caused such an outcry among Italy's European neighbours.

This may all be true but people living in the country or even on the fringes of towns complain bitterly of shots fired at frighteningly close range, of being afraid to go for walks or sometimes even to leave their homes. Cartridge cases, beer or brandy bottles and cigarette packets litter the hunters' favourite haunts.

One friend who frequently protests to the carabinieri and forest wardens gets nowhere. 'Some of them *are* carabinieri and forest wardens!' she complains. Instead she got a bucket of snail poison thrown into her garden, and one of her cats died before she realised what had happened. And this gives a glimpse of a truly vile streak in Umbrian life.

Countless dogs die terrible deaths from eating poisoned bait which hunters put out to kill the foxes that compete for their prey. Our own golden retriever, Maia, who grabbed one at the mouth of a foxhole before we could stop her, would have been among them if our heroic vet Lucia had not abandoned her dinner guests to spend the evening fighting for her life. Rival groups of hunters deliberately poison each others' dogs. 'Recently an area just above here was turned into a hunting reserve,' Tiziano Baldoni, a vet in Castel Ritaldi, near Spoleto, told me. 'Until then, poachers used to have it to themselves – they would go at night to hunt boar, which can bring in quite a bit of money. They didn't like legitimate hunters going after their prey so they put poison bait around to kill their dogs. Between 20 and 30 dogs died on the spot within three months. The same happens with truffle hunters, especially over white truffles for which they are paid so much. When they identify a spot where white truffles grow they put poison around to stop other peoples' dogs finding them.' During a bad year he says he treats between 15 and 20 dogs that have been poisoned 'and all my colleagues will have seen roughly the same number.'

In fact, although public opinion in general has turned against the hunters, there is little that the authorities can do – or more precisely, are prepared to do – to stop any of the abuses. One person who spends a lot of time trying however is Sauro Presenzini. Presenzini is a postal worker but in his free time he leads the World Wildlife Fund volunteers who help police the activities of hunters. 'In the old days people hunted because they were hungry. A man would go out to look for a hare or a pheasant, it would be a free meal. He would use one, maximum two, cartridges. Now hunting is pure consumerism. People shoot anything, just for the pleasure of killing.' Presenzini's thirty trained guards are a drop in the ocean, though, 'there is one of us to 1,500 hunters'. But they are strongly resented. They have had their tyres slashed, their cars deliberately scratched and once a WWF minibus was set on fire. Every so often a bullet arrives in the post, with a note saying 'the next one is for you'.

Then there is the problem of the boar. While driving through the countryside of a weekend, one can suddenly be confronted by numbers of men kitted out in a manner that would make Sylvester Stallone green with envy, carrying big guns and telling you the road is closed. Shouts and shots can be heard all around as others beat noisily through the undergrowth. The wise visitor turns tail and makes off as fast as possible in the opposite direction, for it is boar hunts that claim most casualties – to the extent that the Hunting Federation has instituted courses on safety for chief huntsmen and their assistants. Many boar hunters carry powerful rifles with a range of three or more kilometres, which make environmentalists' hair stand on end but which hunters say are actually safer than smooth-bored guns, partly because the bullets are less inclined to ricochet.

Objectionable though it may be, boar hunting is – or more precisely has been made – an urgent necessity. Having practically wiped out the Italian wild boar, a smallish and relatively harmless creature which produced at the most half-a-dozen offspring a year, some hunters introduced foreign boar from Eastern Europe – huge beasts which, lacking any natural enemies, have been reproducing exponentially, producing two or even three litters of ten or twelve offspring a year. They do an immense amount of damage to crops – 250,000 Euros worth a year, Signor Barbino says, for which the farmers have to be compensated. The agriculture department in the provincial government of Terni calculated that its environment could support no more than 15,000 wild boar. At present, Signor Barbino says, the province has an estimated 55,000.

For all the gunfire in autumn and winter there is no denying that things have improved. One can hear birdsong now, where ten or twenty years ago there was little or none. One can see hares, foxes, pheasants and rare birds again in the countryside. And the barrage of shots on Sunday mornings in autumn is certainly not as intense as it once was.

And this fact may herald an eventual solution. For the number of licensed hunters has plummetted in recent years. Younger people are not attracted by hunting, they have other interests, says Signor Barbino. And, one might add, many have different attitudes to nature and the killing of living creatures. Hunting is becoming an older man's hobby (only a very small number are women), the average age of a hunter now, he estimates, is around 50.

Sauro Presenzini is cautiously optimistic. 'With luck, in ten to fifteen years it should all be over – for lack of primary material.' Not for lack of birds and animals, he means, but of men with guns.

A man was driving along a mountain road one day when he accidentally hit a dog and knocked it unconscious. Being a kind-hearted man – many others would have left the animal by the side of the road – he loaded it in his car and took it to a vet. The vet patched it up and said 'it should be all right now. But this is not a dog, it is a wolf.'

Wolves have been reappearing in Umbria in recent years, although not in large enough numbers to solve the boar problem. They are an endangered and a protected species but, as ever, have a bad reputation. Environmentalists say this is unfair and the attacks on sheep and other damage which mountain farmers protest about is more often the work of packs of abandoned dogs that have reverted to the wild state. But since farmers get compensation for damage by wolves and not for that done by dogs, guess who gets all the blame.

Umbria's wildlife is still remarkable and a walk or even a drive in the countryside can bring encounters with fascinating creatures. Such as, for instance, porcupines – large American-style creatures with fearsome brown-and-white spikes. They are nocturnal and very shy, glimpsed mostly in the light of one's headlights, like small bushes running for cover on ridiculous little legs. An accidental brush with one can end with a flat tyre.

By day one can come across a streak of bright, almost luminous green anything up to 45 centimetres long. It is a ramarro, the biggest and most beautiful of the lizard family around whom many folk myths are woven. Instead of escaping, it will often stand its ground and stare at you – which is how it mesmerises its prey. Highly aggressive (though not to humans) it does not hesitate to take on vipers and other snakes. The males fight brutal territorial battles during the mating season, before mating almost as brutally – raping would perhaps be a better word – with the duller-coloured females.

In the olive groves around various Umbrian towns one can be puzzled by strange rustling noises. A closer look and one is confronted by one or more tortoises charging over the rough ground like small tanks. These tortoises are in a sense a new wild species, an unplanned byproduct of international attempts to ban trafficking of tortoiseshell. Sometime in the 1990s the Italian government banned all trade in tortoises and ordered all owners to register theirs, on pain of hefty fines, the equivalent in lire of between 3,000–9,000 Euros. Whether people forgot to register theirs in time, or simply panicked at the severity of the law, is not clear but many simply dumped their tortoises in the nearest patch of land, and left them to fend for themselves. Fortunately, the tortoises have been living and reproducing happily ever since.

One morning a friend of mine went to his kennel and found both his dogs dead, with clear signs that they had been poisoned. He could not prove it, but he knew it was the work of a neighbouring family who thought he was siding with other neighbours in a dispute. Dog-owners in the suburbs of a nearby town are nervous about even letting their dogs into their gardens, for passers-by have been known to lob poisoned bait into gardens.

Poisoning of people's dogs and cats to spite the owner or simply because they are seen as a nuisance, is by no means limited to hunters. One is reminded once again how close Umbria's primitive past is. The only hope for an end to this shocking and by no means rare practice is that modern civilisation will eventually drive it out. For it is so easy to do, and so hard to prove and prosecute.

In the meanwhile, modern attitudes to nature have brought some remarkable changes. Eight parks and conservation areas, created admittedly on instructions from the national government in the 1990s, are now preserving some of the most beautiful mountain areas: the Monti Sibillini, Monte Cucco, Colfiorito and Monte Subasio, as well as the Valnerina and a long stretch of the Tiber and its valley. It is rare that nature reserves are created artificially, but a splendid and unintended consequence of a dam thrown across the Tiber in 1963 for hydroelectric purposes was the formation of a 500-hectare area of wetlands near the little town of Alviano which immediately attracted a remarkable variety of wildlife. After a huge battle by environmentalists, the area was declared a nature reserve and is now run by the World Wildlife Fund. There, close to the roar of the traffic on the A1, the Autostrada del Sole, is the home or resting place for some 150 species of birds including cranes and white heron (egrets), pelicans and flamingos, where a network of nature trails, gangways, silent electric boats and hides make it a nature-lover's paradise. As are, incidentally, the much smaller nature reserves of Lake Trasimeno and the marsh at Colfiorito.

Living here

So you would like to buy a house in Umbria? As time goes on it is getting harder to find the proverbial dream house, and practically impossible to find it – as one could some forty years ago – for a song. Umbria is by no means the cheapest part of Italy from that point of view. Canny proprietors often hang on to their picturesque ruins for years, watching the prices going up and rubbing their hands at the thought of the pile of gold that await them when they finally decide to sell. If you manage to get your hands on an old house, that is just the beginning: the cost of restoring it can easily be as much as the purchase price, and often several times more. No architect's estimate, however scrupulous and realistic, ever seems to cover the full cost of doing up a house.

'You know I really think people leave their brains at home when they come to buy a house here,' a friend of mine once remarked. I think she was commenting on a single lady who had fallen in love with and was seriously considering buying an old house in the country, miles away from any village or even any other habitation, despite the fact that she did not drive. But there are even quite sensible people who, carried away by their enthusiasm, are prepared to buy houses so decrepit that, if they were in their own countries, they would not even consider them. And very old buildings can cause nasty surprises.

One person I know of decided she would rescue and restore an abandoned 13th-century church that lay, half-buried and full of earth, on her land. She asked an architect friend how much it would cost, reckoned she could just about afford it, they found a good builder and work started. First, while trying to create space between the church and the hillside, they hit rock and needed expensive sledgehammers. Then they found the buried remains of a tiny, much earlier church attached to the bigger one and, carried away by enthusiasm (as were the architect and the builders) – she decided to reconstruct it. Then the repair of the vault called for complex structures and techniques which had not been foreseen. By the time it was finished the costs were three times the original estimate, and the owner was over her head in debt and facing ruin. To survive financially, she would have to sell the place.

No sooner had the builders left than it rained, and rained, and rained. Water poured into the church through the walls and the roof. The place was soaking wet, green and black algae were forming – who would buy the building in that state? Efforts by the builders to improve the waterproofing were only partly successful. It was two years – during which time she had been abandoned by the architect – before she discovered that the cause was simply bad workmanship and sloppy insulation. Once corrected, the problem was solved and the church successfully sold. But the experience – and this is only part of that story – was a major personal trauma. Even now I can take no pleasure in the beauty of that resurrected church – for as you may have guessed, the owner was myself.

I learned many lessons: that one must be ultra-careful and ultra-critical, one must not rely on anyone, even friends, one must get an estimate by a professional surveyor first and that one must try and foresee all possible pitfalls before one starts. But in the end, most people are not in a position to have total control over building work, one has to try and make sure that the people one engages are good at their job. In Italy there is a category of professionals called *geometri* which is something like surveyors, but they are allowed to design, build and renovate buildings. Some are doubtless very good but they do not have an architect's training. Friends of mine entrusted the renovation of an old water mill to a *geometra*. For reasons best known to himself he had a ditch dug around the building, it rained heavily and one wall collapsed, bringing part of the roof with it. Five workmen were in the house at the time, but miraculously none were hurt.

One way of avoiding unwelcome surprises is to buy a house that has already been renovated, if you can find one to your taste. It will seem more expensive but it could well cost less in the end than doing the renovation work oneself.

Other friends of mine, while househunting, found it worthwhile to hire a *geometra* to check carefully for hidden snags to a house. These could be legal, structural or connected with urban planning. They had friends who had innocently bought a house, fairly isolated in the country, only to get first a local dog pound, then a shooting range, set up close by. There is still plenty of unspoilt countryside in Umbria but thorough enquiries into the local council's plans, regulations and, if possible, ethics, are a wise precaution if one does not want to find a large cement works planted outside one's front door one day. An estate agent, needless to say, is not best authority on this. A critical look around the territory of the *comune* would also give an idea of how responsible or environmentally conscious the authorities are. By their fruits shall ye know them.

Buying a dream house does not, of course, mean that the rest of one's life becomes a dream. Real life tends to reassert itself soon enough, starting with the notorious bureaucracy. Nor is Umbria everyone's cup of tea. Two Americans who had settled here, independently of each other, sold up and went back home: they missed the stimulation of their big cities. But most people I know are extremely content and would not dream of moving. If one has the basic requirements for being happy, then Umbria provides some of the best surroundings for happiness that I can think of.